MEDITATE *to* ELEVATE

MEDITATE *to* ELEVATE

HARNESSING YOUR SUPERPOWERS IN A WORLD OF CHAOS

KHALIL MUHAMMAD

New Society Press

MEDITATE *to* ELEVATE
HARNESSING YOUR SUPERPOWERS
IN A WORLD OF CHAOS

Copyright © 2024 by Khalil Muhammad

Book production managed by Zarinah El-Amin of Book Power Publishing

**NEW SOCIETY PRESS books may be purchased in bulk for
educational, business, corporate or sales promotional use.**

For more information, please contact the author:
mrkhalilceo@gmail.com

FIRST EDITION

ISBN 978-1-945873-94-2 (paperback)
ISBN 978-1-945873-96-6 (ebook)
ISBN 978-1-945873-95-9 (hardcover)

Printed in the United States of America

Dedication

I would like to express my deepest gratitude for my beautiful mother, Cynthia Brewer-Williams, who was my inspiration, greatest supporter, and first teacher for practicing a positive mindset. She stuck with me through my most challenging times, and when others couldn't see my vision, she enthusiastically reminded me that, "You can do it." Even up to her last night on earth, our last conversation, she told me to keep preaching to her. She requested this while she lay in bed on the night before her passing. She said, "Khalil, keep teaching, your voice gives me peace."

And to my grandmother, who lives on through me; my intellectual friend, LaTonya who made sure I was sharp; and Fatima who assisted me in my toughest moments, I also dedicate this to you.

To my students, who constantly inspire me with their curiosity and dedication, thank you for being a vital part of my journey.

I pray this helps my "son sons" and those that come after.

And to the rest of my entire family and community, I am so thankful for your support.

Contents

We can become the best version of ourselves.

Meditate to Elevate: Harnessing Your Superpowers in a World of Chaos is a profound exploration of practices that have transformed the author's life and can do the same for you. Drawing from a wealth of knowledge gained from various meditation schools and extensive education, this book is a heartfelt endeavor to share the keys to unlocking inner peace and prosperity.

Khalil Muhammad's intention-fueled journey through life's many changes and challenges led to his discovery of meditation as a powerful tool for healing and transformation. Through mindfulness and meditation, the author found the means to focus the mind, heal from trauma, and manifest abundance, health, and wellness. These profound revelations sparked a sense of duty to offer others the same transformational potential to unlock their inner peace, prosperity, and freedom from societal norms.

For Muhammad, meditation became a path to becoming one's own therapist, a way to check in with oneself, and a means to address internal issues with kindness and clarity. It marked the beginning of a profound shift in life, from a scattered existence to one of control, self-discovery, and freedom from external pressures.

The choice to offer meditation practices to busy city dwellers stems from Khalil's desire to dispel the myths surrounding meditation, which is often associated with remote monasteries and serene seascapes. In reality, meditation knows no boundaries — it can be practiced amidst the hustle and bustle of daily life, whether one wears a three-piece suit or yoga pants. There is no required venue or dress code for mindfulness; it is accessible to all.

This book introduces practical exercises, engaging games, and actionable strategies that serve as effective tools for enhancing focus, clarity, and creativity. The exercises promote the rewiring of the brain through neuroplasticity and build mental muscles to amplify focus not just in the games but in everyday life.

This book is a comprehensive introduction to meditation techniques, including:

- Mindfulness exercises
- Instant stress relievers
- Mental health improvement
- Strengthening clarity and focus
- Understanding mindpower
- Urban nature reconnections
- Breath and body-work
- Visualization techniques
- Healing practices of music and sound
- Manifestation exercises
- Brain reshaping
- Actions to cultivate self-love, gratitude, and inner peace

Meditate to Elevate is a practical resource to expand an already existing repertoire, offering a diverse selection of practices to infuse peace into anyone's schedule.

The fusion of ancient wisdom and modern science is the cornerstone of *Meditate to Elevate's* unique approach. Drawing from timeless teachings and aligning them with contemporary scientific findings, the book provides a holistic view of mindfulness and personal manifestation.

Spiritual aspects of meditation are deeply explored, referencing sacred texts like the Bible, the Quran, and various religious traditions that promote meditation and focus. The book delves into historical practices, revealing their universality and enduring relevance.

The author's personal experiences are shared as proof of meditation's transformative power. He has witnessed its profound effects daily, from coping with intense triggers to regaining inner calm. These experiences offer readers a glimpse into the life-changing potential of meditation.

Author's Note

This book emerged from my experience as a life coach after I came to realize that simply providing information wasn't leading to the desired outcomes of change and healing. Despite my dedication to meditation, I felt compelled to explore additional avenues for growth.

I decided to broaden my understanding by attending mindset conferences and various meditation classes across the U.S., eager to acquire new techniques. It was during this exploration that I shifted my focus from traditional life coaching to the healing potential of meditation. Witnessing the tangible results of this transition was incredibly rewarding and sparked a deep enthusiasm within me.

Motivated by these experiences, I delved into further research and documented my findings in writing. My aim is to share these insights with a wider audience, hoping to assist more individuals on their paths to inner transformation and healing. Let me begin by debunking what I call the 4 myths about meditation.

The Four Myths about Meditation

Meditation, a timeless practice, remains a puzzle for many in today's busy world. Though meditating offers an array of benefits, misconceptions persist, deterring countless souls from embracing its potential. Let's begin with the most widespread myth:

Myth: Meditation is solely for spiritual or religious individuals

While it does hold profound spiritual value, it's an inclusive practice, accessible to everyone regardless of their beliefs. Meditation is essentially a simple method to train the mind, to cultivate focus, serenity, and heightened awareness. Beyond its spiritual connotation, it is a practical tool to alleviate stress, manage anxiety, unlock creativity, manifest desires, refine sleep quality, and amplify both physical and mental prowess.

Myth: Meditation requires substantial time and effort:

Another illusion to dispel revolves around the notion that meditation demands substantial time and effort. However, the reality is that meditation is offered in various forms and lengths, ensuring adaptability to all schedules and preferences.

Myth: Meditation is a breeze!

Conversely, the misconception that meditation is a breeze requires debunking. It's true that meditation isn't a vigorous physical activity, but it necessitates dedication and regularity. The endeavor lies in upholding the practice consistently over time, gradually reaping its benefits.

Myth: Meditation is only for those with easy lives

Lastly, a fallacy surfaces wherein meditation is perceived as exclusive to those leading trouble-free lives. In truth, meditation extends its benefits to all, irrespective of their life circumstances. It's a versatile instrument aiding in stress reduction, enhancing sleep quality, bolstering cognitive function, and more. Meditation doesn't discriminate; it's a practice for everyone's betterment.

Clearing the cobwebs of misconceptions around meditation is pivotal. It's not just for the spiritual, it's not necessarily time-consuming, it's not always effortless, and it's not exclusive to those without struggles. Despite its timeless presence and multifaceted benefits, meditation remains enigmatic.

Consider this an invitation to the curious minds pondering meditation's path. It's not an elitist pursuit, it doesn't demand ceaseless hours, and it's not a cakewalk. Instead, meditation beckons as an avenue for exploration and growth. It's a transformative odyssey ripe with untapped rewards. By dissecting and disarming these misconceptions, we pave the way to an enriched and illuminated life.

SECTION I
Beginning A New Journey Through Meditation Practices

CHAPTER 1
Navigating the Link Between Mind, Body, and Spirit

HAVE YOU EVER found yourself at night, surrounded by your thoughts, and wondered how you ended up here tired, stressed, and disconnected from your core tranquility? You're not alone. In our bustling lives, laden with demands and distractions, it's easy to overlook our inner equilibrium. But consider this—there's a timeless solution, a practice confirmed to ease stress, heighten mental clarity, and foster holistic well-being. Yet, before delving into the mechanics of meditation, let's embark on an exploration of the intricate relationship between the mind, body, and spirit—a trinity often neglected in the pursuit of worldly achievements.

Envision this trinity as a tripod, with each leg signifying a unique facet—mind, body, and spirit. If one leg falters, the entire structure wobbles. Admit it: we have all experienced focusing disproportionately on one leg, neglecting the others. Our fixation on physical appearance has left our minds and spirits yearning for acknowledgment. The truth is, these components are interconnected; they demand equilibrium for true harmony.

Now, address the skepticism: "I'm not spiritually inclined, so can meditation work for me?" Absolutely! Meditation transcends spiritual confines; it welcomes all with open arms. It's about forging a connection with oneself, quieting the mind, and embracing the present moment. Here's the beauty—it's universal. Age, occupation, religious beliefs—none of that matters. Meditation is for every soul.

So, how does meditation function, you ask? Through meditation, you train your mind to focus on the here and now. You release mental clutter — worries, distractions, incessant thoughts. Simultaneously, your body responds. Heart rate steadies, breath deepens, muscles unwind. It's akin to hitting reset for your entire being. But that's not all. Meditation's influence isn't confined to relaxation; it extends far beyond. Research connects it to stress reduction, anxiety alleviation, heightened immune function, and even blood pressure control. And don't overlook cognitive enhancements—enhanced focus, memory, and creativity. It's an investment yielding multidimensional rewards, enriching overall well-being.

Integrating Meditation and Healing for Optimal Well-being

A trove of meditation techniques awaits. Guided meditations, breath-centered practices—the repertoire is vast. The key is to discover what resonates and cultivate consistency. It's crucial to bear in mind that initial challenges are part of the journey. Meditation, like any skill, matures with practice. Let me share a personal insight into how I discovered the power of meditation and healing. While running my floor refinishing company, I learned that I could handle more than just one job a day, and sometimes, even more than two. Everything went smoothly until an employee couldn't make it, a client's schedule shifted, or a machine malfunctioned. In these moments, it was my commitment to excellence and my dedication to delivering on my word that kept me going.

I quickly realized that the first step to overcoming these challenges was to regain control over my thoughts and emotions.

I needed to calm my body and mind, so I could think clearly and strategize effectively. This process involved focusing on my goals, assessing available resources, and visualizing each mission successfully accomplished.

It became apparent that I had the ability to find solutions even when situations seemed impossible. I honed the skill of turning adversity into an opportunity. Yet, the core of my success lay in maintaining a calm and focused mindset, something I accomplished through my ever-growing meditation practices.

But beyond my business experiences, I discovered self-care after realizing the need for balance in my life. Managing my flooring company and organizing events were pressure-filled tasks, demanding a lot of my energy. I understood that self-care was not an option but a necessity for my well-being. My self-care journey has been extensive, encompassing various practices like traveling, massage, yoga, meditation, and exercise. These practices have transformed me, making me more optimistic, reducing stress, and improving my overall health. I became more conscious of my actions and emotions, responding with positivity even in challenging situations.

Meditation became a gift, a tool that allowed me to rewire my mind and become the person I aspired to be, not one shaped solely by societal norms. Mindfulness, on the other hand, taught me the art of being present in both chaotic and calm moments. Incorporating meditation into my daily routine was a significant turning point. I found that it helped me navigate life's complexities with ease. Meditation wasn't just a practice; it was a way of life. The profound shift in my mindset and overall well-being was remarkable.

As we explore meditation and healing practices in these chapters, remember that they are not one-size-fits-all solutions. In your own practice you will find that gradually, the initial unease transforms into ease. Soon enough, you'll find yourself at night, not glued to your screen but enveloped in tranquility. The moment has arrived to prioritize mind, body, and spirit.

Incorporating meditation into your daily tapestry can be transformational. It's not an escape; it's an opportunity to face reality with clarity and composure.

As you tread this path, you'll witness meditation's ripples extend beyond mental and physical well-being. They'll permeate your entire existence—relationships flourish, work gains new dimensions, and the world reveals its intricate marvels. Embracing this journey with open arms, you discover that meditation naturally releases a flow aimed for healing your acquired imbalances.

What Can We Heal Here?

There were many surprising, confusing, and even some upsetting points along my life's journey to work in the healing arts. Looking back from my current mature age, it all adds up, but I can clearly remember a moment of wondering, *Why is this happening to me?*

One day, I was taking a long drive on the interstate highway, enjoying leaving the city behind. Without the interruptions of traffic stops, pedestrians, potholes, and all the other road-based agitations, driving can be very peaceful for me. However, as I was driving, a young member of our community was in the extreme opposite of a peaceful moment. She was threatening to take her own life, and her loved ones were calling on me to come talk her out of it.

While my muscles made automatic moves to turn my car around, my mind spat out a slew of opposing thoughts: *How in the hell am I actually doing this? I'm trying to live my life, they should call the police...*

But the reality was that I was always helping people in their lowest moments. That was and is my role in this life. This situation was just one of many hard times in which I have been sought out to provide solace and support to people from varied walks of life. I have been an adviser to celebrities, clergy, tormented souls, and people on so many different paths. I have been gifted and have developed the ability to talk with people.

How is it that I have the ability to hear what people in pain are trying to say and I can respond with words they can hear back and use? Like they say: "Opinions are like buttholes, everyone has one." So how is that my advice is truly *good advice?*

There have always been beautiful, brilliant, and suffering people around me. From them I was inspired to seek more of the beauty and less of the suffering. I chose to heal myself and, in time, accepted that I was inspiring others. It is a natural cycle in which my healing must beget more healing.

I define healing, as being balanced, and in alignment with your intended self—the being we were each designed to be. For instance, when we love ourselves and have confidence it activates a neurotransmitter associated with pleasure and reward that reduces stress and emotional exhaustion while introducing more feelings of happiness and satisfaction.

Healing allows for constantly being able to see clearly, as decreasing high stress or cortisol levels makes it impossible to see the bigger pictures in life. Within the bigger picture is positivity that can otherwise be obscured as our vision is narrowed by stress, only allowing us to see the negative aspects of situations. Without healing from the unavoidable traumas and challenges each individual uniquely faces, we can't be that super being with an upright nature who we were created to be. Healing helps us be creative, and optimistic, finding ways to navigate whatever life throws at us with an optimistic end goal. To heal, is to activate that spirit of God you were made with and walk in that higher order in every part of our lives.

Meditation isn't about seeking perfection or striving for enlightenment. It's about self-compassion, about dwelling in the present, and about discovering serenity within. It's about thriving in a world overflowing with potential.

CHAPTER 2
Meditations Through Time: From Ancient Scriptures to Modern Celebrities

IN THIS CHAPTER, we begin on a journey to explore the practice of meditation as it has been woven through the fabric of human history. We'll explore how meditation was embraced by figures in religious scriptures, how it's utilized by individuals in the modern world, and how it has shaped religious traditions over time.

There are numerous stories supporting meditation and connecting with God through prayer and fasting as important practices in Christianity. Here are several of my favorites:

- The story of David and his Psalms: David was known as a man after God's own heart, and he used to meditate on God's word and sing Psalms. David is believed to have written many of the Psalms while meditating and seeking God's guidance. In Psalm 1:2, David writes about meditating on God's word day and night. Psalm 46:10, for example, states "Be still, and know that I am God." This verse encourages us to quiet our minds and hearts to be aware of the presence of God. It reminds us that true peace and understanding can only be found in stillness and quiet reflection.

- Another example of meditation and mindfulness in the Bible is found in the book of Joshua, where God commands Joshua to meditate on the book of the law day and night (Joshua 1:8). This verse shows that God values and encourages the practice of meditating on His word and considering it deeply. It is a reminder that spending time in quiet contemplation and reflection can help us to better understand and follow God's will for our lives.

- In addition to David and Joshua, many other figures in the Bible, such as Jesus and Paul, also practiced meditation and mindfulness. Jesus often withdrew to quiet and solitary places to pray and reflect (Matthew 14:23), while Paul wrote about the importance of having the mind of Christ (1 Corinthians 2:16). These examples demonstrate that meditation and mindfulness are not only beneficial but also essential for developing a deeper relationship with God. They remind us that taking time to quiet our minds, focus on God's word, and listen for His guidance is an important part of the Christian faith.

- The practice of meditation and mindfulness can also be seen in the teachings of Jesus. In Matthew 6:6, Jesus encourages his followers to "go into your room, close the door and pray to your God, who is unseen." This passage highlights the importance of finding solitude and quiet to connect with God. It is a reminder that to truly hear the voice of God, we must first create space for Him in our lives.

- In the book of Philippians 4:8, Paul writes "whatever is true, whatever is noble, whatever is right, whatever is pure, whatever is lovely, whatever is admirable—if anything is excellent or praiseworthy—think about such things." This verse highlights the importance of mindfulness and awareness of our thoughts. It reminds us that by meditating on positive and uplifting thoughts, we can cultivate a mind that is in line with the teachings of Christ.

- Meditation is central in the story of Moses and the Burning Bush. Moses was a prophet of God who received the Ten Commandments from God while meditating. According to the Bible, Moses was on a mountain, where he encountered the burning bush, which was God's presence. He was meditating and fasting for 40 days and nights before God called him to lead the Israelites out of Egypt (Exodus 3:1-4:17).

- Meditation was also pivotal in the story of Elijah and the Still Small Voice. Elijah was a prophet of God and a miracle worker who was running from Queen Jezebel. He was in a cave on Mount Horeb, waiting for a sign from God. After a great wind, earthquake, and fire, God revealed Himself to Elijah in a still small voice, which Elijah heard while meditating (1 Kings 19:9-18).

- In the Bible, Jesus is seen meditating in the Garden of Gethsemane before they intended to crucify him. This story is found in Matthew 26:36-46. Jesus went to the garden to pray and meditate before facing the greatest trial of his life. While in the garden, Jesus asked God to take away the "cup of suffering" that he was about to face. His meditation in the garden was a demonstration of the power of prayer and meditation to bring us closer to God. Through this story, we are reminded that even when facing great trials, we can still take time to meditate and pray to God for guidance and comfort.

These stories demonstrate that meditation and connecting with God through prayer and fasting is an important practice in Christianity that has been valued by Christians for thousands of years.

By meditating on God's word and spending time in quiet contemplation, we can deepen our understanding of God's will for our lives and strengthen our relationship with Him. It is also important to remember that meditation and mindfulness are not just practices for monks or spiritual leaders but can be incorporated into our daily lives to stay connected to God and find peace within the chaos of life.

More Monotheism

- Looking at Islam we see the story of the Prophet Muhammad and the Cave of Hira. The Prophet Muhammad (peace be upon him) used to spend time in the Cave of Hira, where he would meditate and receive revelations from Allah (God in Arabic). It is said that the first verses of the Quran were revealed to him during one of his meditations in the cave.

- There are stories from the Quran that demonstrate the importance of meditation and deep focus, as a means of connecting with Allah and receiving guidance and revelation. Just like the other prophets who frequently sought out or had opportunities for solitude, the Prophet Muhammad also used solitude and meditation to deepen his connection with Allah.

Modern Meditation

Contemporary public figures sometimes share how they manage the stress of busy lifestyles coupled with constant scrutiny. The following individuals are known to practice meditation and have shared their experiences with the public, helping to make meditation more mainstream.

- **Oprah Winfrey:** talk show host, producer, author, actress, and media proprietor, is a well-known meditation advocate and has spoken about the benefits of meditation on her show and in interviews. She practices Transcendental Meditation and has credited it with helping her to find inner peace and tranquility.

- **Russell Brand:** comedian and actor, is a vocal advocate of meditation and has spoken about how it has helped him to overcome addiction and improve his mental health. He practices Transcendental Meditation and has even hosted a podcast on the subject.
- **Gisele Bündchen:** supermodel, is a well-known practitioner of Transcendental Meditation. She has spoken about how it helps her to manage stress and anxiety and to stay focused and energized.
- **Katy Perry:** pop star, is a vocal advocate of Transcendental Meditation and has spoken about how it has helped her to manage stress and anxiety.
- **Ellen DeGeneres:** TV host, is known to practice meditation and has spoken about its benefits for mental health and well-being.

Black celebrities in the rap and sports industry model that meditation is not limited to certain cultures or professions, but rather can be applied to any person from any background. Kendrick Lamar - well-known rapper, J. Cole - rapper and songwriter, and Ryan Coogler - film director and producer, have all spoken about their practice of meditation and how it helps them stay focused and manage stress. They have credited meditation with helping them be more creative and to find inspiration.

Recognizing the scope of individuals who utilize meditation practices, it becomes abundantly clear that meditation is not confined to any particular faith or period in history. Instead, it is a universal practice that transcends boundaries and connects individuals to their inner selves and the Divine, regardless of their religious or cultural background.

Meditation serves as a timeless bridge that unites humanity's quest for inner peace, self-discovery, and spiritual connection. As we journey through this exploration of meditation's abundant offerings, we are reminded that its benefits are not limited to any one group, culture, or era. Instead, they are accessible to all who seek a path toward greater clarity, serenity, and enlightenment. In the pages that follow, we will continue to unravel the threads of this practice, weaving together a tapestry of wisdom and insight from around the world.

CHAPTER 3
The Art of Self-Reflection

IN THE JOURNEY of self-discovery, one of the most profound tools at our disposal is self-reflection. It serves as a gateway to understanding our thoughts and emotions, offering the potential for positive transformation in our lives. Throughout this book, we'll delve into the art of self-reflection, exploring its potential to foster growth and healing. Exploring these pages, you'll discover that self-reflection isn't merely about gazing at oneself but embarking on a voyage of self-acceptance, acknowledging your strengths and vulnerabilities. We will delve into how to embrace your emotions, navigate your thoughts, and leverage them to enhance your life.

Understanding Self-Reflection

Self-reflection, as a practice, involves contemplating and examining our own thoughts and emotions. It invites us to revisit our experiences and comprehend their impact on our being. By scrutinizing our inner workings, we can unearth insights into our behaviors and motivations, making strides toward positive change.

The path of self-reflection isn't without its challenges. There can be unease in confronting our innermost thoughts and emotions. A memory might resurface, illuminating an alternative way to handle a past situation. Nevertheless, it's vital to recognize that self-reflection is a potent catalyst for both personal development and healing. Confronting our fears and uncertainties empowers us to embrace ourselves and our journey.

The Benefits of Self-Reflection

The rewards of engaging in self-reflection are manifold and include:

- Enhanced Self-Awareness: Peering into our thoughts and emotions enriches our understanding of who we are and what we seek. This newfound knowledge fosters self-awareness, offering empowerment. As you identify your core values, passions, and aspirations, your choices can be aligned with these facets of your identity.
- Elevated Emotional Intelligence: Self-reflection deepens our comprehension of our emotions, nurturing emotional intelligence. This heightened awareness equips us to navigate complex situations and relationships with finesse. The journey entails recognizing your emotions, comprehending them, and leveraging them to forge connections with others.
- Amplified Self-Compassion: Self-reflection leads us to embrace our imperfections, nurturing self-compassion. By extending kindness to ourselves, we curtail feelings of shame and guilt, fueling confidence and resilience. Embracing who you are sets the stage for growth.
- Strengthened Relationships: Understanding our behaviors and motivations through self-reflection is pivotal in enriching our interactions. By deepening our self-awareness, communication improves, and empathy thrives. This results in more meaningful connections and fortified relationships.

Crafting Effective Self-Reflection Practices

To reap the full potential of self-reflection, it's paramount to create an environment conducive to introspection. This might entail seeking out a tranquil space where you can be solely at one with your thoughts. Designating specific periods during your day for self-reflection, such as the dawn or dusk, can further enhance the practice.

Utilizing prompts or journaling can be beneficial in guiding your self-reflection. Prompts offer direction to your thoughts, prompting inquiries such as "What did I glean from this experience?" or "What emotions am I experiencing now?" Journaling allows you to chronicle your sentiments and musings over time, serving as a personal narrative through which you can trace your progress.

Another crucial approach is to face self-reflection with an open heart and a yearning to learn. Anticipate revelations about yourself that may take you by surprise, and be receptive to transformation. Remember that self-reflection is a dynamic process, woven through various encounters and emotions that reshape your understanding of yourself.

Furthermore, practicing honesty with yourself is pivotal. As you navigate the realm of self-reflection, authenticity, and vulnerability are crucial. It's tempting to avoid or sugarcoat certain emotions or thoughts, yet true self-reflection requires the courage to confront even the most challenging aspects of ourselves. These often hold the most potential for growth and healing.

Integrating feedback from others also stands as a valuable aspect of self-reflection. External perspectives can illuminate blind spots and biases. Seek out observations and insights from individuals you trust and respect, weaving their wisdom into your self-discovery journey.

Finally, remember to extend grace to yourself and nurture

self-compassion. The voyage of self-reflection is both demanding and emotional, and it's crucial to remember it's a journey, not a destination. Embrace your achievements along the way and refrain from fixating solely on setbacks.

My Self-Reflection Practice

In my personal journey, meditation acted as a powerful revealer of hidden truths within me. Amidst moments of stillness, as my thoughts flowed through my mind, I grounded myself, observing my thoughts and external world without reacting. This practice, honed over time, cultivated an inner strength, enabling me to navigate life's challenges more adeptly. While my personal and family history is marked by chaos that was detrimental during my formative years and intermittently thereafter, eventually my path became one of learning and transformation. My exploration of self unfolded as I delved into my inner landscape, aligning myself with profound understandings that guided me toward practicing balance in my life.

My journey did not unfurl without constant external molding and inspiration. Amid financial struggles and stresses that come with urban living, my unwavering faith in prayer coexisted with my more intellectual quest for self-understanding. It's very likely that my maternal uncle did me an immense favor by instilling in me a curiosity in the sciences. I'm not even sure if my young uncle wanted a little tagging along with him to his classes at Wayne State, maybe he was just forced to babysit, but he created core experiences with me during my trips to his university. Watching him work in chemistry labs and doing serious science work spoke directly to my autodidactic nature.

My lifelong pursuit of knowledge has extended into neuroscience studies, where despite not attaining a degree, my endeavors were propelled by self-awareness for healing myself and others rather than traditional career aspirations. Among the tapestry of my inner programming, I unraveled the indoctrination of societal preconceptions, gradually becoming more illuminated by meditation. Through a lens of self-reflection, I armed myself with insights to navigate life's challenges, transforming them from burdens into catalysts for growth.

Being single was uniquely triggering to me and was connected to a hesitation to face my deepest thoughts and emotions. Fears of loneliness and leaving an untold legacy would swirl within me. But then, I discovered the comfort of living in the moment, realizing that being alone doesn't have to mean feeling lonely. The realization that we are never truly alone, and the significance of self-love transformed my experience. While companionship would have been cherished during those moments, I discovered the richness of my own company.

In the busy city life, being able to quiet the external noise and tune into my inner rhythm has been an essential roadmap on my journey. Discovering insights from the unseen yet profound laws governing our existence has helped me find tranquility amid the hustle and bustle of the city. These universal laws, intricately woven into the fabric of our existence, serve as my anchor amidst the urban chaos. To those on their own journey, I encourage you to immerse yourself in these unseen principles, letting them harmonize your path.

CHAPTER 4
Images and Their Impact: Navigating the World of Visual Influence

I MAGES HOLD A remarkable power to mold our thoughts, emotions, and perceptions, shaping our very existence. Being a visual artist and practitioner of meditation has uniquely positioned me to help others combine the tools of visualization and meditation for personal growth.

In a prayer to God, I asked for a way to uplift and assist those around me. What followed was a remarkable testament to the profound impact of images—a meditation revealed to me in a dream. I am reminded that this wasn't just a mere dream but a direct gift from the Creator.

This experience unveiled the potential of images as more than just visual constructs. They possess the ability to be a conduit through which God answered my prayer, sparking change and purpose within our lives. It was this very image that spurred me to forge an unbreakable bond with my entrepreneurial spirit, driven by a relentless passion to empower others with life-changing opportunities.

Furthermore, my path led me to embrace the role of a meditation and mindfulness teacher. Through this journey, I unearthed the true essence of mindfulness—not just as a tool for self-awareness, but as an anchor against the chaos of external opinions and influences. This was my sanctuary, shielding me from distractions and enabling me to remain steadfast in my commitment to my divine mission.

Growing up in challenging circumstances, I was blessed with a natural understanding of visualization. My ability to envision positivity amid adversity has become my guiding light, illustrating how we can shape the reality we hope for. These early experiences stand as a testament to the potency of images in shaping our narratives.

The stories I share here are an embodiment of the profound impact external images and projections towards us can have on our journey. It is a story of divine revelation, personal transformation, and the potent coalescence of the spiritual and the visual. Just as I embraced the meditation gifted by God's answer to my prayer, I encourage you to discover the transformative potential of images in your own lives.

In honoring the divine connection that unfolded within my journey, we embark on a compelling exploration of the intersection between images and spirituality. Through introspection and mindfulness, we will uncover the extraordinary influence images wield, molding our paths, and forging connections between the seen and the unseen.

CHAPTER 5
The Healing Symphony of Nature

NATURE HAS ALWAYS held a profound allure for me. The serene embrace of water, the soothing rustle of leaves, and the grandeur of the outdoors have etched vivid memories in my heart. When I was young, my grandmother made sure I went camping. Those days, far from the bustling city life, forged a profound bond between me and the world around me. Amidst the absence of towering buildings and urban imagery, my attention naturally turned inwards, fostering a journey of introspection that began to unravel the layers of my true self.

As a teenager coming from the inner city, the camping at various spots around Michigan impacted me forever. Imagine experiencing the chaos and glaring violence of living in a gang populated neighborhood, and barely ever seeing a tree or a pond. When I first saw the enormous oak and the maple trees everywhere, it was like I was transported to another world.

I remember one tree - a log really - laying across rushing water, and we had to walk on it to get across. I couldn't swim a lick. I was never exposed to anything like this kind of environment before, no one could have even given us kids a heads up of what to expect. My instincts did not align with this new world, so this is when I had to go into myself and focus. I had to be present or fall into the water. Back then I feared water, and I was afraid of heights, so I was petrified. When I made it across, I realized I had something unknown within me. There was a toolbox that I could dig around in and use when times were challenging.

Once we arrived at a safe space in the woods, we pitched a tent and I learned to build a campfire. I enjoyed imagining how people used to actually live in these conditions at one point of time. My mind would veer away from the tough city life and relax into these visualization exercises. Just as urban living did, the all-encompassing environment of being in the woods demanded my full attention, yet the difference in my feelings was remarkable. Stress just seemed to evacuate my body and oh how I enjoyed the peacefulness and beauty of that moment.

The water was full of particles from the forest, and in some areas, you could see the water flowing past the campsites. We slept in tents that we had pitched and increased our outdoor skills with each new experience.

Let me not forget to mention snakes. This one park not only had snakes, but we also actually cooked one and ate it. This was another thing that was so foreign to my inner-city experience but was more natural to my grandmother and elders who had prior opportunities to do things like fish, hunt, and forage. Eating snake did not stick as a habit for me, but I remain thankful for such intimate connections with the natural world.

Those moments camping allowed me to connect with myself in ways I could never have imagined in my concrete jungles. At such a young and pivotal age, camping would be a part of my real introduction to the practice of not only being present, but also to using mindfulness techniques (which I still had no name for) to connect with the environment and quiet my mind's fears. This deeper connection unveiled the essence of nature's impact on the human spirit. The uninterrupted immersion in the natural world was akin to stepping into an alternate reality, one where my being resonated harmoniously with the earth's rhythm.

Spending time in nature reveals unlimited gifts within us as we are surrounded in an abundance of divine creation. Each leaf, every rustling sound, was a reminder that I was part of a larger tapestry woven by divine hands. The enchanting harmony of nature's symphony was evidence of a higher order, an order that spoke volumes about the presence of a Creator guiding every facet of existence.

This awareness gradually evolved into a profound understanding of the intricate universal laws that govern our world. I began to perceive the handiwork of God in every detail, a reflection of divine wisdom that orchestrates the very essence of nature. My connection with nature, rooted in the wisdom of these laws, became a guiding light in navigating the complexities of urban life. As towering skyscrapers overshadowed the greenery, I found solace in knowing that these laws transcended the physical realm, permeating every corner of existence.

The serenity I experience by the water or in the heart of an architected park is a testament to the enduring bond I share with nature. It is a bond enriched by my understanding of the divine laws governing the universe, a bond that allows me to find peace amid the chaos of urban life. Nature's canvas is where I find renewal, but it is the underlying harmony of God's design that truly ignites a sense of tranquility within me. Nature's teachings, imprinted with the wisdom of universal laws, serve as a guidepost, inspiring me to live a life aligned with the grand symphony of creation.

CHAPTER 6
Weaving Nature into City Life.
Creating an Urban Oasis

I'VE MENTIONED HOW growing up, my affinity for nature was nurtured through camping excursions that my grandmother orchestrated. It was during those moments, far from the confines of urbanity, that I felt an indescribable connection with the world around me. The transformational impact of those early encounters with nature led me to question how I could integrate its wisdom into my urban lifestyle.

Urban life, with its bustling streets and towering edifices, can often seem worlds apart from the serenity of nature. Yet, amidst the concrete jungle, lies a realm of opportunity to cultivate a profound connection with the healing power of the outdoors. For me, as I navigated through life, I found myself drawn to bodies of water. Eventually, I made the decision to create a life where living by the water was not just a luxury, but a commitment to my well-being. It was a decision fueled by a deep yearning for the tranquility and renewal that only nature can provide.

Living on the waterfront, a conscious choice, has allowed me to bridge the gap between the city's pulse and nature's tranquility. The gentle ebb and flow of the water resonates with my spirit, reminding me of the harmony that exists within the natural world.

I've also found solace in urban parks, where pockets of

greenery offer a sanctuary from the urban hustle. The urban landscape, infused with pockets of nature, serves as a reminder that even amid man-made structures, the natural world continues to thrive.

I've been fortunate to bridge these two worlds, weaving nature's embrace into my city life and reaping the rewards of physical, mental, and spiritual well-being.

Reflecting on the divine laws that govern every aspect of nature, I realized that these laws extend beyond the boundaries of the wilderness and into the heart of the city. They are a constant reminder that the universe operates with precision and purpose, and it is our privilege to harmonize our lives with this grand design. Nature's laws are a gift that allow us to navigate the urban maze with a sense of balance and mindfulness.

Guided by these insights, I've discovered that urban living need not be a departure from nature, but an opportunity to strengthen our connection with it. The bustling streets and towering buildings may contrast nature's tranquility, yet they provide a canvas upon which we can weave moments of natural wonder. By integrating elements of nature into our urban spaces, whether it's a potted plant on a windowsill or a mindful walk through a park, we forge a bridge between two worlds that often seem divergent.

So, to those seeking a harmonious blend of urban dynamism and natural serenity, I offer this advice: Uncover the wisdom of the unseen universal laws that underpin nature's majesty. Recognize that these same laws extend to the city, inviting us to embrace them as guiding principles in our urban lives. Engage in a practice of mindfulness, allowing the gravitational pull of nature's wisdom to lead us towards equilibrium. With consistent meditation and a heart open to nature's teachings, you'll find a profound understanding of the delicate balance that enriches both urban and natural realms.

CHAPTER 7
The Power of Visualization

V ISUALIZATION IS A potent practice that enables us to craft mental images and scenarios, propelling us towards positive change and attaining goals. Through the art of imagination, we wield a powerful tool capable of honing our focus, amplifying motivation, and dismantling limiting beliefs.

Evolving Thoughts via Imagination

Our minds are always sending us information in the forms of thoughts. Many of us just take the thoughts and react to them as if they are truth and even direction. I use my daily dawn ritual to fully harness the potential of visualization, with my precise intent being key to the outcome. Instead of conjuring vague concepts of desires, we must strive to paint vivid mental images, capturing each intricate detail of our aspirations. Aim to focus so that you are visualizing only the things that you want to regain control over in your life. Put aside all of the interference and noise for these few moments.

I begin this first meditation of the day while my mind is slowly waking up amid a low, alpha brain wave state (being wakeful but relaxed). I start by reminding myself that every-thing that my mind's eye "sees" came from within me, by God's permission. Everything in God's divinely ordered universe, including matter and energy is made up of subatomic particles without any physical structure. Everything, including thoughts, emit vibrational frequencies. Through this meditation, I aim to align my thinking and feeling using my imagination at the same vibrational frequency.

I like it when my mind is a little foggy and tired, because I want this experience downloaded into my subconscious mind where it becomes cemented for recall. In this meditation, I practice imagining my desired reality until it becomes my true reality. I am aware that I have the power of things subservient to me, as God intended for them to be. God has made everything usable to the human family for the period of time we are here on this earth. When we align our thoughts, focus, and the feelings in our body, we shape the world around us, creating what we desire.

Things in this world are not really the way we imagine that we see them, they are really energy in constant flow and change. So, in my drowsy sleepy state, I mentally look around the perimeter of my home. I'll follow the flow of the connected walls from room to room all the way around the house until I come to my bedroom where I lay. I then expand my exploration beyond my dwelling's confines, mental gazing over my city. In this relaxed meditative state, I am allowing my physical eyes to rest, even though they will naturally move behind their lids, as I embrace the architectural tapestry with the eyes of my mind.

I recognize that each structure and street originally stemmed from human vision and inner contemplation. This revelation affirms to me that the entirety of my perception and all existence is birthed from within us—my reality is entirely within me. I acknowledge our human potential as creators, with the Divine's benevolence overseeing it all. I continue seeking with my mind's eye to perceive even the most concealed facets. Widening my view to the expanse of my state, I draw my vision out, panning to look at the sun. I peer all the way around the immense star, then pan to the moon. I don't have to toil to create this visualization exercise, I can connect with it, because the imagery and myself are the same "energy." I am in what is commonly known as a flow state.

After a short time of such an expansive outer view within my mind's eye, this metaphysical journey delves deeper, penetrating the very core of my being. I begin to scan my entire body. From the top of my head to the inside of my head around my brain, I will look around my eyes, then look closely at the skin and details of my face.

As I tread this inner realm, I invoke the remembrance of the boundless creativity I observed earlier. I reinforce the idea that creation burgeons from within. Each step along this intangible path rewires my inner self, etching a potent reminder: I am a creator, an orchestrator of manifestation. This meditative visualization technique extends seamlessly to my aspirations, infusing them with Divine order and quantum reality, harmonizing my intentions with the cosmos. After these moments of focused meditation, I will be equipped to better manage the ebb and flow of my thoughts. I have built this idea of what I desire in my mind, so I will hold it even through my days and nights, not allowing other false realities appear as thoughts in mind.

I do this visualization exercise until I have scanned my entire body, including an audit of my muscles, heart, and gut. My view is an energy that I can freely use to "look" at every cell of my vessel. When I have completed this last portion of my visualization, called a Body Scan Meditation, I will lay for a few short minutes feeling the connected power that everything within and outside of us shares. Then I open my eyes.

Once I stand up and begin moving through my day, I see the interconnectedness of all things. I no longer see things as separate or out of reach for me. Everything I need and desire is accessible to me.

Over time, I've cultivated an array of meditative practices. These exercises are accessible to others through my website, motivationalmuseum.com. Visualization, for me, transcends technique; it stands as my cornerstone. Through this practice, I have ascended, surpassed, and evolved, all under the watchful eye of the Divine.

Here is a grounding and calming visualization exercise you can do for anywhere from five to thirty minutes.

Visualization Meditation Instructions:

1. Find a quiet and comfortable place to sit. Close your eyes and take a deep breath in through your nose, filling your lungs with air.
2. Exhale slowly through your mouth, letting go of any tension or stress in your body.
3. Imagine yourself in a peaceful and relaxing place. This can be a real or imagined place. It could be a beach, a forest, a garden, or any other place that brings you peace and calm.
4. Take a moment to notice all the details of the place. Notice the colors, sounds, smells, and sensations. Imagine yourself walking around the place and taking it all in.
5. If your mind wanders, gently bring your attention back to the visualization and continue to take in the details of the place.
6. Continue this practice for 5-10 minutes. When you are finished, take a moment to notice any changes in your body and mind before opening your eyes.

CHAPTER 8
Understanding and Balancing the Body's Energy

WITHIN LIFE'S INTRICATE web, the interplay of energy has captivated the minds of scientists, practitioners, and individuals across the ages. The body's energy systems, intricate as they are, can be categorized into the nervous and endocrine systems. Recent scientific insights have illuminated pathways toward nurturing equilibrium, fostering our overall health and well-being.

These systems, intricately intertwined, coalesce to shape our existence. The nervous system orchestrates its dance of electrical impulses, facilitating our movements, sensations, and responses. Conversely, the endocrine system acts as a master chemist, conjuring hormones that govern vital bodily functions such as growth and metabolism.

To unlock the secrets of the body's energy equilibrium, we must first comprehend the interdependent relationship between these systems. Their harmonious interaction begets homeostasis, bestowing us with optimal health and vitality. Yet, when the scales tip, a cascade of consequences ensue. Stress, an unwelcome companion, disrupts the delicate equilibrium. The nervous and endocrine systems falter, giving rise to stress hormones, impairing our ability to cope. The repercussions are profound, spanning emotional turmoil to physical ailments.

Mitigating stress and championing relaxation form the bedrock of energy equilibrium.

Techniques like meditation and deep breathing offer respite amidst life's tumult. The rhythmic cadence of inhales and exhales becomes a soothing elixir, calming the storm within. In my own journey through the urban sprawl, deep breathing serves as my compass to tranquility. With each breath, the knots of stress unravel, replaced by a serenity that echoes within.

Exercise, a vital facet of this equilibrium, unfurls as a pathway to liberation. Through activities like walking, swimming, cycling, or weightlifting, we engage in a dance that releases endorphins, unburdens stress, and heralds relaxation. This seemingly simple act empowers us to navigate life's currents with grace and vitality.

Time management, a stalwart guardian against burnout, enters the fray. An organized, structured routine shields us from chaos, granting clarity and tranquility. And within this mosaic of well-being, sleep emerges as a cornerstone. A dearth of slumber disrupts the delicate partnership of the nervous and endocrine systems. Rest becomes the salve to restore harmony.

In the grand tapestry of well-being, understanding and balancing the body's energy remain a lifelong journey. Guided by holistic practices, we chart a course toward equilibrium – from relaxation to nutrition, from exercise to time management. By nurturing ourselves, we conduct symphonies of well-being, directed by the baton of balance.

Prioritizing self-care becomes the chorus of our existence. Amidst the whirlwind of obligations, moments of meditation, leisurely strolls, or contemplative reading bestow precious fragments of calm. In the cadence of a bustling day, scheduled breaks provide sanctuary, an opportunity to stretch and rejuvenate, shedding tension's grip. With each inhalation, tranquility is summoned, infusing our beings with vitality.

Nutrition, a culinary alchemy, forges the elixirs of equilibrium. A diet rich in fruits, vegetables, whole grains, and proteins fortifies our bodies, ensuring that the engines of energy hum in harmony. By bypassing the allure of processed foods and tempering our consumption of sugar, caffeine, and alcohol, we further augment our vitality.

As we navigate life's intricate paths, embracing these practices, we tap into an abundant wellspring of energy. In these simple yet profound acts – from deep breaths to nourishing meals – we reclaim our vigor, harmonizing our energies with the cosmic rhythm.

CHAPTER 9
Decluttering

CLUTTER IS EASILY misunderstood as the mess of the careless. In reality, driven and passionate people easily fall victim to the clutter that can accumulate in the wake of their endeavors. Under the heavy load of managing multiple businesses, I found myself juggling tasks and commitments, inadvertently allowing chaos to infiltrate my surroundings. Books, documents, and personal items were always scattered everywhere– a reflection of my busy life. This is a common problem with entrepreneurs whose personal and business spaces frequently overlap. Owning an art business comes with managing many cumbersome pre- and post-production materials, as does my hardwood flooring company.

Before I appreciated the art of decluttering, in addition to all the paper trails of receipts and work orders I must manage, there would be infinite art and flooring supplies, such as polyurethane cans, Duraseal stain charts, and tools bouncing around in my truck. Rushing from one place to another, my various environments mirrored the growing turbulence within. I was also teaching meditation classes and taking various meetings between my messier, hands-on work. When I was running behind, I would change in my truck, adding my sanding clothes to the mix.

As the external clutter grew, the chaos seeped into my mental realm. I was going mad. My possessions amassed haphazardly, and my focus waned in the midst of visual distractions. A general sense of unease settled in, and I was regularly frustrated when locating things I needed became a task. Then anxiety mounted as tardiness became routine, and the impact on my psyche was palpable!

It was during my journey to declutter that I grasped the transformative power on my internal well-being based on whether I neglected or maintained an external order. I remember coming home and noticing the difference of keeping my space organized with placing things where they should go opposed to the times when I left things laying around in disarray. Having it neat and organized left me feeling at ease. The same with my vehicle. I appreciated it more when it was cleaned inside.

I peripherally knew about these "clutter versus decluttering" theories from studying various things in my meditation journey, and decided to take a closer look. What I learned reflected exactly what I had been personally experiencing. With disorganization came unclear focus, decreased productivity, and reduced my mental health. Clearing my physical chaos led to newfound mental clarity. Organizing my surroundings restored a sense of purpose, offering tranquility to my state of mind.

My outer transformation yielded inner changes. The guilt tied to clutter dissipated as belongings found their place. Self-esteem surged, and my surroundings evolved into havens of authenticity, fostering a positive self-image.

Decluttering transcended the physical and emotional. Clarity outside translated to clear decision-making within. As external chaos abated, so did internal turmoil. Distinguishing between essentials and non-essentials became natural, reducing procrastination and aligning me with my aspirations.

Decluttering transformed me. External order birthed internal clarity, calming my spirit and enhancing punctuality. Just as I had read about how the universe, nature, and all function in an orderly fashion, I decided that's how I prefer to be in alignment, like the rest of creation. My newfound mental space empowered me to serve others better, enriching interactions and presenting the best version of myself. Decluttering emerged as a well-being conduit, harmonizing the external and internal.

CHAPTER 10
How to Use Physical Movement to Promote Healing and Balance

OVEMENT IS ESSENTIAL to our well-being, both physically and mentally. According to science, regular physical activity can help improve cardiovascular health, strengthen bones and muscles, and reduce the risk of chronic diseases such as heart disease and diabetes. But did you know that movement can also be used as a tool for inner healing and psychological restoration? In this chapter, we will explore the scientific evidence behind the connection between movement and healing.

The human body is designed to move, and physical activity can help promote the flow of blood and oxygen throughout the body, which is essential for healing and maintaining good health. When we move, we stimulate the release of endorphins, which are chemicals in the brain that act as natural painkillers and mood elevators. Regular physical activity can also help reduce inflammation in the body, which is a key factor in the development of many chronic diseases.

In addition to its physical benefits, movement can also have a positive impact on mental health. Exercise has been shown to reduce symptoms of depression and anxiety and can also help improve cognitive function and overall well-being.

In my own journey, I discovered the profound power of movement in promoting healing and balance. Just like my physical environment became cluttered, amidst the hustle and bustle of managing multiple businesses and constantly rushing from one meeting to another, I often neglected my physical well-being. Incorporating regular physical movement into my daily routine became a powerful tool for promoting healing and balance.

However, it's important to understand that not all movement is created equal. To truly promote healing and balance, it is essential to engage in a variety of different types of physical activity, including both aerobic and strength-training exercises. A balanced approach that includes cardio, strength training, and stretching is ideal.

Additionally, the importance of posture and alignment cannot be overstated when it comes to promoting healing and balance in the body. Poor posture and alignment can lead to chronic pain, muscle tension, and even respiratory problems. Conversely, good posture and alignment can improve overall function, reduce the risk of injury, and promote healing and balance.

The spine serves as the foundation of the body, and maintaining proper alignment reduces stress on the joints and muscles. Achieving this can be accomplished through exercises that target core muscles like the abdominals and back.

Equally vital is the alignment of the hips and pelvis, which form the foundation of the lower body. Proper alignment in this area reduces stress on the lower back, hips, and knees. Exercises focusing on strengthening the hip and thigh muscles, such as squats and lunges, contribute significantly to this alignment.

Incorporating exercises that emphasize posture and alignment into daily life can effectively promote healing and balance. However, remember that posture and alignment should be integrated into all aspects of your life, not limited to exercise.

CHAPTER 11
Mastering Your Brainwaves

THE HUMAN BRAIN emits different types of electrical waves, known as brainwaves, which correspond to different states of consciousness. These brainwaves can be measured using an EEG (electroencephalography) machine, which records the electrical activity of the brain. Understanding the different types of brainwaves and how to control them can help us to improve our memory, creativity, and overall well-being.

The five main types of brainwaves are:

1. **Gamma waves** (30-100 Hz): Gamma waves are associated with high levels of cognitive processing and are present during states of alertness and high-level information processing. They are also present during states of high-level creativity and problem-solving.

2. **Beta waves** (13-30 Hz): Beta waves are associated with normal waking consciousness and are present during states of active problem-solving, decision-making, and logical thinking. They are also present during states of anxiety and stress.

3. **Alpha waves** (8-12 Hz): Alpha waves are associated with a relaxed state of consciousness and are present during

states of deep relaxation, meditation, and visualization. They are also present during states of creativity and intuition.

4. **Theta waves** (4-8 Hz): Theta waves are associated with deep relaxation and are present during states of deep meditation, creativity, and intuition. They are also present during states of sleep and dreaming.

5. **Delta waves** (0.5-4 Hz): Delta waves are associated with deep sleep and are present during states of deep sleep and unconsciousness.

To be in peak states during all these brainwaves and derive better memories, creativity, and overall well-being, there are several techniques that can be used:

- **Meditation** is an excellent way to control brainwaves and enter a state of deep relaxation. By practicing mindfulness and concentration, we can slow down our brainwaves and enter an alpha or theta state, which can help to improve creativity and intuition.

- **Progressive Muscle Relaxation** (PMR) is a technique that involves tensing and relaxing different muscle groups in the body in a specific order. This can help to relax the body and mind and promote a sense of calm.

- **Exercise** is an excellent way to control brainwaves and enter a state of alertness and focus. By engaging in regular physical activity, we can increase our gamma and beta brainwaves, which can help to improve cognitive function and decision-making.

- **Getting enough sleep** is essential for controlling brainwaves and maintaining overall well-being. During sleep, our brainwaves slow down and enter a delta state, which is necessary for deep, recovery sleep and memory consolidation.

- **Listening to music** can also help to control brainwaves and enter a specific state of consciousness. Music with a tempo of 60-80 beats per minute can help to slow down brainwaves and enter an alpha or theta state, while faster-paced music can help to increase gamma and beta brainwaves.

Understanding the different types of brainwaves and how to control them can greatly improve our quality of life in various areas such as emotional, financial, spiritual, mental, and physical well-being. Creating a routine that incorporates different techniques for controlling brainwaves can be an effective way to improve our overall quality of life. It is important to get enough sleep for controlling brainwaves and maintaining overall well-being.

CHAPTER 12
The Power of Sound Healing

SOUND HEALING IS the practice of using sound to assist in healing and homeostasis within your body. It is based on the idea that sound can have a powerful effect on the body, mind, and spirit. This is supported by scientific research, which has shown that sound can have a positive effect on the nervous system, immune system, and overall well-being.

I may not have directly participated in formal sound healing sessions, but I have found solace and healing through the intentional use of sound in my life. Whether it's the resonating frequency of 432 Hz, the spiritually uplifting recitation of the Quran by Noreen Mohammad Siddiq and Omar Hisham, or the soothing melodies of Mozart, these sounds have served as powerful tools for my mental and emotional well-being.

There have been moments when the stresses of life threaten to intrude on my peace, and in those instances, I turn to the harmonious vibrations of sound. The recitations by Siddiq and Hisham, in particular, hold a special place for me, transporting me to a serene mental space. Even in the midst of a busy workday, the gentle embrace of Mozart's compositions through my earphones has provided a positive escape, redirecting my focus from subconscious concerns to a more conscious state of balance.

As a spiritual being, my commitment to regular meditation and other healing practices generally keeps me grounded and stress free. However, when challenges arise, the transformative power of sound becomes a valuable ally in restoring equilibrium to my mind and spirit.

The Healing Power of Music

Music therapy is one of the most well-known forms of sound healing. The use of music to achieve specific therapeutic goals, such as reducing stress and anxiety, improving mood, and reducing pain. Research has shown that music therapy can be effective in treating a wide range of conditions, including depression, anxiety, and chronic pain.

Music has been used for healing for thousands of years, and modern science has confirmed the therapeutic benefits of music. Music can be used to reduce stress, anxiety, and pain, and improve mood and cognitive function.

Listening to music can activate the release of endorphins, the body's natural painkillers, which can help to reduce pain and improve overall well-being. It can also have a positive effect on the cardiovascular system, by slowing the heart rate and reducing blood pressure.

Music can also be used to promote relaxation and sleep. Listening to calming and soothing music before bedtime can help to relax the mind and body, making it easier to sleep and stay asleep.

The Healing Power of Mantras

Another form of sound healing is the use of mantras. Mantras are sacred sounds or words that are repeated as a form of meditation. For thousands of years in various spiritual and religious traditions, mantras are believed to have a positive effect on the mind and body. Recent research has shown that the repetitive use of mantras can lead to a decrease in stress and anxiety, as well as an improvement in mood. This is thought to be since mantras can help to focus the mind and reduce distractions, leading to a state of deep relaxation.

Mantras can also be used to promote physical healing. The vibrations created by the repetition of mantras are believed to have a positive effect on the body and can be used to help treat conditions such as chronic pain, hypertension, and diabetes.

In all sound healing practices, it is important to make sure that the sound you're listening to is of high quality and does not cause any discomfort or harm to the ears.

In addition to music and mantras, there are other forms of sound healing that can be used to promote healing. One example is the use of singing bowls or tuning forks. These instruments are struck or played to produce a specific frequency of sound, which is believed to have a positive effect on the body. Another example is the use of nature sounds, such as the sound of waves crashing or birds singing. These sounds are believed to have a calming and relaxing effect on the mind and body and can be used to promote deep relaxation and restful sleep.

Ancient Practices of Sound Healing

In ancient civilizations such as Egypt, Greece, and China, sound healing was used as a form of medicine to promote healing and balance in the body. In ancient Egypt, the sound of the sistrum, a musical instrument like a rattle, was believed to have healing powers and was used in religious ceremonies and healing rituals. The ancient Greeks also believed in the healing power of sound and used music and song in their healing practices.

In traditional Chinese medicine, the use of sound healing is known as "Qigong" and it's based on the belief that sound vibrations can help to balance the body's energy, known as Qi or Chi. This practice includes singing, chanting, and the use of musical instruments such as the gong. In ancient India, the practice of sound healing is known as "Nada Yoga" which uses sound and mantras to bring balance to the body and mind.

In many indigenous cultures, the use of singing, chanting, and drumming are still used in healing rituals and ceremonies.

In all these ancient cultures, sound healing was a powerful tool that could be used to promote healing and balance in the body. The specific techniques and instruments used may vary from culture to culture, but the underlying belief in the healing power of sound is a common thread throughout history.

Sound Healing Practices for Everyday

Here are some sound healing practices you can do throughout your busy day:

- **Humming:** Humming is a simple and easy sound healing practice that can be done anytime, anywhere. It involves making a humming sound with the mouth closed. This can help to promote relaxation, reduce stress, and improve overall well-being.

- **Tongue Trilling:** Tongue trilling is another simple sound healing practice that can be done anytime, anywhere. It involves making a trilling sound with the tongue by rapidly vibrating the back of the tongue against the roof of the mouth. This can help to improve the flexibility of the tongue and reduce tension in the jaw, neck, and shoulders.

- **Solfeggio Frequencies:** Solfeggio frequencies are a specific set of frequencies that are believed to have healing properties. Listening to these frequencies can help to promote relaxation and improve overall well-being. You can find Solfeggio frequency tracks on the internet and listen to them through your phone or any device.

- **Chanting:** Chanting is a simple and easy sound healing practice that can be done anytime, anywhere. It involves repeating a word or phrase, such as "Om" or "peace," in a rhythmic manner. Chanting can help to promote relaxation, reduce stress, and improve overall well-being.

- **Singing:** Singing is an easy sound healing practice that can also be done anytime, anywhere. You don't need to be a great singer to experience its benefits, singing any song that you like or even humming a tune can help to promote relaxation, reduce stress, and improve overall well-being.

Sound healing is a powerful tool that can be used to promote balance in the body. Whether it's through music, mantras, or other forms of sound, the healing power of sound is undeniable and worth exploring as a means of promoting overall well-being.

When you dive into these transformative exercises, don't concern yourself if it feels a bit odd at first. After all, what's truly strange is choosing to endure life's challenges without taking proactive steps to enhance your quality of life. Remember, it's not about how anyone else perceives it either; it's about your journey to becoming the greatest version of yourself and gaining the clarity you seek in life. You are not embarking on this adventure alone as millions of people across time have benefitted from these practices. In my own practice as a meditation coach, I have witnessed hundreds of people evolve their lives through these various practices. Together, we will unlock the fullness of our potential and embrace a more profound and fulfilling existence.

CHAPTER 13
Regaining Control: Strategies for Reclaiming Autonomy and Achieving Personal and Professional Goals

MANY OF US go through life feeling as if we are in control of our own destiny. We make plans, set goals, and work towards achieving them. However, there are times when we may feel as if we are being controlled by outside forces, making it difficult to reach our intellectual, physical, spiritual, and financial targets in life.

One of the most obvious signs that we are truly the one being controlled is when we find ourselves constantly making decisions based on the opinions and wishes of others, rather than our own. We may feel as if we cannot decide without the approval of someone else, or that we must do things a certain way to please others. This can be especially true in relationships, where we may feel compelled to do things to please our partner or avoid conflict, even if it goes against our own values, wishes, and desires.

Another sign of being controlled is when we feel as if we have no autonomy or agency in our own lives. We may feel as if we are just going through the motions, without any sense of purpose or direction. We may also feel as if we are constantly being told what to do, whether by a boss, a parent, or a partner. In these cases, it can be difficult to take the initiative and make decisions for ourselves, leading to a sense of powerlessness and frustration.

Feeling trapped or confined in one's situation is also a sign of being controlled. We may feel as if we have no options or that our choices are limited, leading to feelings of hopelessness and despair. This can be particularly true in situations where we may feel as if we have no control over our financial or career situation, or where we feel as if we are being held back by societal expectations or stereotypes.

In my personal journey, I never felt like I was giving away my power because I was sure of myself and had confidence in what I believed in. I was strong against peer pressure because I had knowledge of self, and I strived to gather the right information needed to propel me towards my goals. Entrepreneurship was my path, and I didn't let anyone dictate otherwise. Some family and friends suggested pursuing a traditional 9-5 job, but I remained focused on building my company. Even during challenging times, I didn't rely on anyone else's finances, choosing the path of struggle and maximizing what resources I had until my provision increased.

When we are being controlled, we may also feel a sense of disconnection from our own bodies and emotions. We may find ourselves numb or detached and may struggle to connect with our own feelings and desires. This can be especially true when we are being controlled by others who may be using manipulation tactics.

To regain control of our own lives and reach our intellectual, physical, spiritual, and financial targets, it is important to recognize the signs of being controlled. By becoming aware of these signs, we can take steps to break free from the control of others and make decisions that align with our own values and desires.

Reclaiming our power and taking control of our own lives can be a challenging process, but it is essential for achieving our intellectual, physical, spiritual, and financial goals.

Here are some strategies that can help us reclaim our lives and assert our autonomy:

Journal Reflection

Take a moment to sit quietly and reflect on your current circumstances. Ask yourself:

- Are my decisions driven by my own desires and values, or do I find myself constantly seeking validation from others?
- Do I feel a sense of autonomy and agency in my life, or do I often feel like I'm just going through the motions?
- Am I setting boundaries to protect my autonomy, or do I frequently find myself succumbing to external pressures?
- Do I believe in my own ability to shape my destiny, or do I feel constrained by limiting beliefs?
- How connected do I feel to my own thoughts, feelings, and desires?

Take a few deep breaths and allow yourself to sit with these questions without judgment. Notice any emotions or sensations that arise. Write down your responses in a journal to gain clarity and insight into your current level of autonomy.

Boundary Setting Visualization

Close your eyes and visualize yourself surrounded by a protective bubble or aura. Imagine this bubble as a boundary that separates you from external influences and pressures. See yourself confidently asserting your boundaries when faced with situations that threaten your autonomy. Envision yourself standing firm in your decisions, rooted in your own values and desires. Feel the strength and empowerment that comes from honoring your own needs and priorities.

Practice this visualization regularly, especially before challenging interactions or decision-making moments. Allow yourself to embody the sense of autonomy and empowerment that comes from setting and maintaining healthy boundaries.

Values Clarification Exercise

Take some time to identify your core values and priorities in life. Ask yourself:

- What matters most to me in my personal and professional life?
- What are my non-negotiables when it comes to my relationships, career, and personal well-being?
- How do I want to be remembered and what legacy do I want to leave behind?
- Create a list of your top values and priorities and rank them in the order of importance to you. Use this as a guide when making your decisions and goal-setting to ensure that your actions are aligned with your deepest values.

By practicing, you can have a deeper understanding of your own autonomy and take more solid and well-intended steps towards taking back control over your life. Self-awareness is everything in this journey, as well as the courage to honor your own truths and not just flow where the wind blows.

CHAPTER 14
Controlling Anxiety in Everyday Life

Living with anxiety can be incredibly overwhelming and debilitating. It can make it difficult to focus, to make decisions, and to keep up with everyday tasks.

When I was making a pilgrimage to Mecca and visiting other countries, it was my first time ever on a plane. The ticket was in the thousands of dollars, and I ordered it even though I greatly feared heights. The day came, and "overwhelming" was an understatement of how I felt. I knew there was no turning back once it was time for takeoff.

A surprising thing happened once I was seated. From the seat behind me, a man began to massage my shoulders. I looked back, and it was my friend! We had coincidentally booked the same trip. It was a truly comforting twist of fate.

At that moment, I had to confront my anxiety head-on. The thoughts of fear began playing in my head, making the situation feel even more daunting. My friend said some good, positive words to me, but I realized that I had to pep talk myself. I had to stay in contact with myself, reminding myself that the thoughts of fear were not real. They were simply generated because of my fears, and I needed to find a way to overcome them. Fortunately, I had already learned some exercises to stomp out my anxious feelings.

There are many techniques you can use to gain control over anxiety and live a happier, more fulfilling life.

Here are six steps you can take towards finding control over anxiety in your everyday life:

1. **Identify Your Anxiety Triggers:** The first step to finding control over your anxiety is to identify the triggers that cause it. This can be anything from certain situations, people, or even certain emotions. Once you know what triggers your anxiety, it will be easier to find ways to manage it.

2. **Challenge Your Negative Thoughts:** Anxiety often comes from negative thoughts or beliefs. Taking time to challenge those thoughts can help you gain control of your anxiety. Ask yourself questions such as, "Is this thought really true?" or "What evidence do I have to support this thought?" This will help you to separate the truth from the lies and help you to gain control over your anxiety.

3. **Practice Self-Care:** Self-care is an essential part of building self-confidence and dealing with anxiety. Taking time to do things that make you feel relaxed and happy, like reading, going for a walk, or listening to music, can help to reduce your anxiety.

4. **Learn Relaxation Techniques:** Learning relaxation techniques such as deep breathing and progressive muscle relaxation can help to reduce the physical symptoms of anxiety. Taking time to practice these techniques can help you gain control over your anxiety.

5. **Seek Social Support:** Anxiety can make it difficult to connect with others, but having strong social support can help you manage your anxiety. Reach out to family and friends and let them know how you are feeling.

6. **Take Care of Your Body:** It is important to take care of your physical health when dealing with anxiety. Eating a balanced diet, getting regular exercise, and getting enough sleep can all help to reduce your anxiety.

Living with anxiety can be difficult, but it doesn't have to be that way. By taking the time with these steps - identify your triggers, challenge your negative thoughts, practice self-care, learn relaxation techniques, seek social support, and take care of your body - you can gain control over your anxiety and live a happier, more fulfilling life. Anxiety is a difficult thing to live with, but with the right strategies, you can find the control you need to lead a more peaceful life.

If you should quickly need it, you can also find this anxiety-reducing exercise at the back of this book.

CHAPTER 15
The Importance of Self-Care: Nurturing Your Body and Mind

SELF-CARE IS NOT a luxury; it's a necessity for maintaining physical and mental health. It encompasses a wide range of activities, including physical, emotional, and mental self-care. The significance of self-care cannot be overstated.

Self-care comes in various forms worldwide. In Japan, self-care is often associated with the practice of "forest bathing," while in India, comprehensive Ayurveda practices take the lead. In Sweden, it's embedded in the tradition of "fika," which is a sort of elevated coffee break. These practices, deeply rooted in their respective culture, aim to reduce stress and promote well-being. The key takeaway is that self-care has long and vastly been recognized as essential, and you must find what resonates with you and incorporate it into your routine.

While juggling our busy work and family lives, self-care may seem like a daunting commitment. However, it doesn't have to be. There are small, manageable practices you can incorporate into your daily life to promote healing and well-being. Practicing mindfulness is one of these practices and can be a powerful tool.

Mindfulness for Self-Care

Here are some step-by-step methods for integrating mindfulness into your self-care routine:

1. Start with a Simple Mindfulness Exercise: Focus on your breath. Sit in a comfortable position, close your eyes, and notice the sensation of the air moving in and out of your nose and mouth without trying to change your breath in any way.

2. Incorporate Mindfulness into Your Daily Routine: Find moments throughout your day to be mindful, like when taking a shower, cooking, or doing the dishes.

3. Make Mindfulness a Part of Your Workday: Dedicate a few minutes each day to focus on your breath or try a walking meditation during your lunch break. This can help to reduce stress and improve productivity.

4. Explore Mindfulness-Based Stress Reduction(MBSR): Consider a program that combines mindfulness practices with yoga and meditation, which has proven effective in reducing stress and enhancing well-being. Look for MBSR programs in your area or try an online program.

5. Practice Mindfulness with Loved Ones: Bond and relax with your loved ones through guided meditation or simply sitting in silence, focusing on your breath.

Remember, mindfulness requires patience, consistency, and a non-judgmental attitude. The more you practice, the more you'll be able to be mindful in different situations and experience its numerous benefits.

CHAPTER 16
Are Your Thoughts Your Own?

SELF-REFLECTION IS THE process of taking time to look closely at your thoughts, emotions, and experiences. It is an important aspect of self-discovery and personal growth. By gaining insight into your thoughts and emotions, you can promote healing, increase self-awareness, and make positive changes in your life.

I discovered the transformative power of self-reflection when I embarked on a journey to become a meditation teacher. During this pursuit, I delved deeper into the workings of my mind and uncovered profound insights.

One of the most eye-opening revelations was that many of my thoughts were not a reflection of my true self. It is a common misconception that our thoughts reflect who we are as individuals. However, the truth is that our thoughts are not ours, they are simply tools that we use to navigate the world around us. Understanding this concept can be crucial for maintaining good mental health and well-being. I, too, once held this misconception about being my thoughts. Like many, I was conditioned to believe that emotions were a weakness, and success was derived from suppressing them, focusing solely on logic and reason.

However, my journey toward understanding the fallacy of this belief began when I embarked on the path to becoming a meditation teacher. It was during this time that I started to become more attuned to what was transpiring within my own mind.

To further my understanding, I delved into various sources, ranging from the wisdom of esteemed neuroscientists to the inspirational teachings of figures like Dr. Joe Dispenza, Napoleon Hill, and Tony Robbins.

Among the practices that resonated deeply with me was mindfulness. It became an essential tool for maintaining the clarity of my mind. I yearned to unearth my authentic self beyond the cacophony of distractions, external influences and thoughts that were not my own. Practicing mindfulness allowed me to listen to the whispers of my inner self and realign my life in the direction I truly desired.

To safeguard my mental space, I made deliberate choices in my daily life. I significantly reduced my exposure to television and mainstream media, recognizing their potential to condition and manipulate my thoughts and emotions. My approach to social media became mindful, too. I meticulously pruned my online environment and carefully curated the content I allowed into my digital realm, aware of the subconscious impact of images and advertisements. By intentionally planting seeds in my mind that aligned with my dreams and aspirations, I began to take control of my thoughts, steering them toward the life I wanted to create.

This awakening brought forth a pivotal realization—my thoughts were not a fixed reflection of my true self. They were malleable, and I possessed the power to reshape them intentionally. I questioned why I should follow a program of inherited thoughts that had nothing to do with my true self and decided to rewrite my thought patterns.

The shift in my thought patterns, in turn, influenced my emotions. I began to choose and focus on thoughts that I wanted to manifest, rather than impulsively overreacting to every passing thought. This newfound sense of control over my thoughts and emotions was liberating, and it set me on a transformative journey of self-discovery and personal growth. I questioned the program I had previously unwittingly followed and pondered where it might have led me had I not intervened. This transformation also had a profound impact on my emotions. I chose the path of calmness and focus over impulsive reactions to every thought that did not truly belong to me.

CHAPTER 17
Embracing Emotional Intelligence

EMOTIONAL INTELLIGENCE IS the ability to understand, manage, and express one's emotions in a way that is healthy and beneficial for oneself and others. Embracing emotional intelligence can lead to greater healing and well-being in our lives.

My own journey led me to appreciate the significance of emotional intelligence. I discovered that the initial step in embracing this skill is becoming acutely aware of our emotions. This means paying meticulous attention to how we feel and precisely identifying the emotions coursing through us. I embarked on this journey by observing not only my emotions but also the physical sensations they produced—the rapid heartbeat, the fluctuating breath, and the changing body temperature.

Once we acquire this awareness, the next step involves mastering the management of our emotions. It's about gaining the skill to regulate our emotions, so they don't spiral into overwhelming or debilitating states. This is where techniques like deep breathing, mindfulness, and cognitive-behavioral therapy come into play. These tools grant us greater insight into our thoughts and feelings, allowing us to mold them in ways that enhance our overall well-being.

Equally vital is the capacity to express our emotions in a healthy manner. This entails honest, direct, and respectful communication of our feelings while also validating the emotions of others. It lays the foundation for building deeper, more meaningful connections with those around us, fostering compassion and understanding.

My own transformation became apparent when I recognized the balance between emotional and logical intelligence. This equilibrium enabled me to succeed not only in my career, but also in nurturing my emotional well-being. I realized that suppressing emotions merely sowed the seeds of future problems. Understanding and managing them, on the other hand, became the key to my well-being and happiness.

As I walked this path, I became a living testament to the power of emotional intelligence. My career thrived, and I also tended to my emotional health. I became a beacon, guiding others toward understanding the vital role emotional intelligence plays in leading a fulfilling life.

Here are six practices that may help you enhance your emotional intelligence amid the hustle of daily life:

1. **Incorporate mindfulness techniques** into your daily routine, such as mindful breathing exercises, mindful eating, or mindful walking.

2. **Practice active listening** when communicating with others. Provide your full attention and make an effort to understand their perspective.

3. **Develop stress-management strategies** like exercise or taking brief breaks to clear your mind.

4. **Cultivate empathy** by attempting to see situations from others' viewpoints and understanding their feelings and experiences.

5. **Prioritize self-care** by taking care of your physical, emotional, and mental well-being through activities like getting adequate sleep, maintaining a healthy diet, and engaging in leisure activities that bring you joy.

6. **Use daily check-ins** with yourself to reflect on your emotions and process any feelings that have arisen throughout the day.

Remember that nurturing emotional intelligence is an ongoing process that requires practice, self-awareness, and patience. Incorporate these steps into your daily routine and make them habitual, ensuring they have a permanent place on your daily to-do list.

Even amidst the chaos of an urban environment, where the daily grind can be overwhelming, these steps can be your allies. You can simplify mindfulness, breaking it into manageable fragments. Micro-meditations, for instance, can be practiced during brief moments of respite throughout your day. It might involve just taking a few deep breaths, perhaps even while stuck in the elevator on your way to the office. Your colleagues might think you're simply daydreaming.

Nature breaks are another option. Take a moment to sit on a park bench or gaze at a tree. Especially in an urban jungle, connecting with nature, even briefly, can rejuvenate your spirit. Maintain connections with loved ones. Reach out to friends and family. They will appreciate hearing from you.

Self-care should always be a priority. Consider indulging in a bubble bath with essential oils to relax and be present in the moment. If you find yourself overwhelmed, do not hesitate to seek support from a life coach. They are like personal trainers for your emotions, assisting you in working through your feelings and devising a plan to manage them.

Improving emotional intelligence in the midst of a bustling and stressful life is possible with a bit of creativity. Remember that emotional intelligence is a skill that necessitates time and practice to develop fully. Be patient with yourself and carve out space in your life for these practices.

CHAPTER 18
Building Mindfulness Through Meditative Practices

WHEN I STARTED my journey into mindfulness and meditation, it was akin to embarking on a fitness regimen for my mind. Much like the dedication I put into weightlifting to build physical muscle, I diligently practiced mindfulness meditation to strengthen my mental and emotional faculties.

Through this practice, I gradually became more aware of the repetitive, stressful thoughts that had once plagued my mind. These whispers of worry, I realized, were often shackled to past events. My growing awareness through meditation was much like the feeling of looking in the mirror to gauge muscle gain during weightlifting. It allowed me to witness my progress as I became more attuned to my inner world.

Mindfulness meditation, combined with my newfound knowledge about emotional intelligence, significantly impacted my life. I started noticing the often-repeated stressful thoughts and whispers of worry. Through meditation, I learned that these thoughts were often connected to past events, and I could be more present in the now. In essence, I was shutting down those old, unproductive thoughts, much like redirecting my weightlifting efforts for maximum results.

As I expanded my awareness through mindfulness meditations, I began to recognize that I had been living in the past, reacting to events that were long gone. It was as if I was driving down the road of life, constantly looking in the rearview mirror. Through this practice, I realized that I could take the power away from those old, debilitating thoughts that had held me back.

Emotional Intelligence

This newfound awareness led me to incorporate emotional intelligence into my life seamlessly. I started addressing issues within myself that had previously gone unnoticed. For example, I learned to identify when I was tired, lacked sleep, or had consumed the wrong foods, which could trigger irritability. This irritability might have initially appeared to be caused by slow drivers on the road or other external factors.

However, I could now trace it back to its actual source, addressing it from within. It was like gaining the ability to check the engine of my car when it started making strange noises, rather than merely reacting to the noise itself.

Gratitude

Cultivating gratitude, an integral part of my life, had a tangible, positive impact on my physical, mental, and financial well-being. My daily gratitude meditation allowed me to not only express gratitude but to feel it deeply within my body. Each day - either in the morning as soon as I wake and am still partially asleep or when I'm slightly sleepy at bedtime - harnessing just ten minutes in these alpha brain wave states is indispensable to my well-being.

Daily gratitude practice is like giving my entire being a tune-up, much like the meticulous care one might give to their car to ensure it performs optimally. This practice not only flushes out negative thoughts but also brings a smile to my face. The act of recalling what I was grateful for feels like clearing away the debris from my mental road, making my journey through life smoother and more joyful.

Journaling

Journaling was another tool I used to declutter my mind and establish order in my life. This act of transferring my thoughts onto paper was immensely liberating. It was like cleaning out a cluttered closet, making space for things that truly mattered. The act of writing released pent-up mental energy, allowing me to allocate my mental resources more effectively, just as cleaning my physical space helped me organize my life.

Forgiveness

Finally, forgiveness, a challenging yet transformative process, was essential. Using emotional intelligence also meant learning to forgive, both myself and others. I realized that forgiveness wasn't just about the other person; it was about releasing the grip of anger, resentment, or hurt that was holding me back.

This practice was about letting go of the negative energy associated with anger or other violations. It didn't mean I had to accept or condone those actions, but I could release the hold they had on my inner self while protecting my own well-being.

It was like cutting the anchor that was preventing my ship from sailing freely. I could be empathetic and understanding while still safeguarding my inner self.

CHAPTER 19
The Healing Power of Journaling

JOURNALING, LIKE MEDITATION, was a transformative tool on my path to self-discovery and healing. It allowed me to organize the jumbled mess of thoughts, emotions, and memories within my mind. As I delved deeper into journaling, I discovered its versatility.

Stream of Consciousness Journaling is much like a mental brain dump, providing an outlet for my racing thoughts. It helped me get those jumbled thoughts out of my head and onto the page, creating a sense of mental clarity and relief. It was like unclogging a drain, allowing my thoughts to flow freely.

Gratitude Journaling became a daily ritual, where I recorded the things I was grateful for. This practice wasn't merely about listing blessings but about genuinely feeling gratitude in my core. It shifted my focus towards the positive aspects of my life, dispelling negativity and promoting a sense of contentment. It was like tending to a garden, nurturing the seeds of positivity.

Emotions Journaling acted as my confidant. I poured my thoughts and feelings onto the pages, especially during challenging times. It was an avenue for understanding and processing my emotions, often leading to profound self-discovery. It was like having a heart-to-heart conversation with a trusted friend.

Dream Journaling brought the ethereal world of dreams into tangible form. I documented my dreams, both literal and metaphorical, unraveling hidden meanings and gaining deeper insights into my subconscious mind. It was like deciphering cryptic messages from my inner self.

Through journaling, I experienced transformative signs. After journaling sessions, I often found myself calmer, more centered, and better equipped to navigate life's challenges. It provided me with a comprehensive understanding of my thoughts, emotions, and personal growth. It became a lifeline during difficult situations, allowing me to work through and process experiences that would have otherwise been overwhelming. Journaling, in essence, was my compass, guiding me through the twists and turns of my inner world.

CHAPTER 20
The Power of Forgiveness

FORGIVENESS, A SUBJECT deeply rooted in my personal journey, holds profound healing potential. I've witnessed firsthand how harboring anger and resentment can manifest physically and emotionally. It was like carrying a heavy burden that slowly eroded my well-being.

Recognizing the negative emotions and the hurt I was holding onto was the first step towards forgiveness. It required acknowledging the pain and the emotional shackles that were preventing me from moving forward. I had to acknowledge this persistent thorn in my side, the source of ongoing discomfort.

Seeking understanding, I attempted to comprehend the motivations and circumstances behind the actions of those who had wronged me. It was a perspective shift, allowing me to see that people are often driven by their own struggles and experiences. I tried to don their shoes for a moment and see the world through their eyes.

Letting go of the need to be right was liberating. I realized that holding onto resentment wasn't worth sacrificing my own well-being. It wasn't about excusing or justifying their actions, but about prioritizing my peace and happiness. Relinquishing this heavy anchor allowed me to sail freely.

Using empathy became a bridge to forgiveness. Trying to understand the violator's perspective fostered compassion. I realized that we're all flawed humans on our respective journeys, often stumbling along the way.

I allowed myself to feel the hurt. Instead of suppressing or denying my emotions, I embraced them. I gave myself permission to mourn—acknowledging the pain, and gradually releasing it. It was an essential step towards healing. Finding forgiveness in my heart was a profound realization. It wasn't about forgetting the past; it was about finding peace and moving forward. Unlocking this door that had been jammed for years, revealed a path to liberation.

Self-forgiveness was equally crucial. Recognizing my own imperfections and mistakes allowed me to extend forgiveness to myself. Reconciling with my inner self and letting go of self-blame and guilt was pivotal. Dwelling on past grievances only hindered progress. It was like cutting the straps that attached me to an old, heavy backpack, allowing me to step into a lighter, brighter future.

Seeking support, whether from a life coach, a friend, or a family member, was invaluable. Sharing my feelings and my journey towards forgiveness provided much-needed solace and guidance—like having a trustworthy companion on a challenging trek.

Acting upon forgiveness was the final step. Making a conscious effort to forgive and actively working towards healing allowed me to embrace inner peace and happiness. It was like crossing the finish line of a long, arduous race, finally finding the serenity I had sought.

Incorporating these steps was transformative. It wasn't a sign of weakness but rather a testament to strength and resilience. Forgiveness, in the end, was a powerful tool for personal growth and empowerment, releasing the negative emotions that had once held me captive. It was a pathway to freedom, both for myself and those I forgave.

CHAPTER 21
Gratitude Unveiled

GRATITUDE, AN ESSENTIAL practice of some of the greatest individuals in history, is scientifically proven to enhance physical and mental health, fortify relationships, and drive personal growth. Just as Aristotle, the ancient Greek philosopher, emphasized the importance of gratitude in living a virtuous life, many influential figures throughout history have recognized its profound impact.

Gratitude, scientifically grounded and historically revered, became the cornerstone of my personal growth journey. Research reveals that it's intricately linked to improved sleep, lower blood pressure, a bolstered immune system, and reduced symptoms of depression, anxiety, and stress. Gratitude isn't merely a sentiment; it's a catalyst for tangible physical and mental well-being.

To harness the power of gratitude, consider implementing these five strategies into your daily routine:

- **Keep a gratitude journal:** Dedicate a few minutes each day to jot down things you're grateful for. It can be as small as a beautiful sunset or as significant as robust health. Reflecting on these aspects enhances your focus on life's positives.

- **Express gratitude:** Share your gratitude with others. Whether through a heartfelt conversation or a simple thank-you note, expressing your appreciation strengthens relationships and deepens connections.

- **Practice mindfulness:** Be present in the moment, appreciating the blessings in your life. Mindfulness aligns with gratitude, allowing you to savor the richness of your experiences.

- **Reflect on the past:** Recall the good things that have graced your life and the people who've contributed to your journey. Reflecting on past blessings amplifies feelings of gratitude.

- **Incorporate gratitude into everyday life:** Seamlessly infuse gratitude into your daily routine. Take a moment to appreciate even the smallest joys, like a warm cup of tea or a friendly smile from a stranger.

Cultivating Appreciation

Appreciation isn't just a fleeting emotion; it's a transformative force. Appreciation, scientifically grounded and historically revered, is your gateway to an enhanced life. It has been practiced by some of the greatest individuals in history, not just for its emotional benefits but also for its psychological and physical advantages. Scientifically, appreciation has a compelling foundation. Research reveals that it's intricately linked to improved sleep, lower blood pressure, a bolstered immune system, and reduced symptoms of depression, anxiety, and stress. It's a catalyst for tangible physical and mental well-being. Appreciation is the key to living life fully, savoring the richness of each moment.

CHAPTER 22
The Universality of Meditation: A Global Journey

EDITATION, A PRACTICE embraced worldwide, transcends cultural boundaries and has been an intrinsic part of diverse societies for centuries. Its applications span from healing and relaxation to spiritual growth. This chapter embarks on a global journey, spotlighting meditation's significance across various cultures and its adaptability to modern, fast-paced lifestyles.

In some African societies, meditation intertwines seamlessly with tradition, often accompanied by movement, music, and chanting. Here, meditation serves as a conduit to connect with the spiritual realm, fostering self-insight and an enhanced understanding of the world.

In Japan, Zen meditation, known as Zazen, takes center stage. This meditation style emphasizes posture, breath control, and mental focus to attain a state of serenity and insight. Meanwhile, in China, the practice of Qi Gong melds movement, breath, and meditation to bolster physical and mental well-being. Integrating meditation into daily life may seem challenging, yet it is entirely feasible. Meditation is flexible, molding itself to your schedule and preferences. Allocating a dedicated time each day, even if only a few minutes, can render meditation more accessible.

Your already established morning and evening routines

present excellent opportunities to begin incorporating a meditation practice. You can try many different ways to fit meditation into your day. For instance, seize moments during your morning coffee preparation or work breaks to meditate. Incorporating mindfulness into daily activities, such as walking or cooking, can also foster a heightened sense of presence.

Meditation is a practice that beckons everyone, transcending age, gender, and background. It offers a tailored experience, adaptable to individual preferences. While some may experience immediate benefits, others might require time to realize meditation's advantages. Patience and perseverance remain key as you traverse your meditation journey.

The healing potential of meditation is vast, spanning stress and anxiety reduction, inner peace cultivation, and overall well-being enhancement. By ardently following a step-by-step guide, embracing different meditation forms, maintaining consistency in practice, and nurturing self-awareness, you can tap into meditation's transformative capabilities. Your journey to well-being unfolds, guided by your dedication to this ancient practice, revered across the globe.

Exploring the diverse facets of global meditation practices, we recognize that meditation is a truly versatile tool. It can be tailored to your unique life circumstances, regardless of your financial or ethnic background. Meditation doesn't require expensive equipment or exclusive spaces; all you need is a quiet corner and your willingness to explore your inner self.

Furthermore, meditation isn't an elitist practice. It's not reserved for a select few. It's an inclusive practice that welcomes all, irrespective of age, financial status, or cultural heritage. Meditation is a democratic path to well-being, accessible to anyone willing to embark on the journey.

As you delve deeper into your meditation practice, remember that progress may vary from person to person. Just as diverse cultures have embraced meditation in their own ways, individual experiences with meditation can differ. Some may find immediate relief from stress and anxiety, while others may require more time and dedication to unlock its full potential. The key is to remain patient and persistent, knowing that meditation's benefits will gradually reveal themselves.

Regardless of where you come from or where you're headed, meditation accompanies you on your journey to well-being. It's a universal companion, offering solace and insight to all who seek its wisdom. As you step onto this global path of meditation, remember that you carry with you the collective knowledge of countless individuals who have found healing, peace, and understanding through this ancient practice. Your journey is enriched by the wisdom of cultures worldwide, connecting you to a shared human experience of seeking well-being and balance.

SECTION II
Body Work

CHAPTER 23
Mind-Body Connection: Unlocking Optimal Health and Well-being for Free

THE MIND-BODY CONNECTION, a multifaceted concept, underscores the intricate interplay between our mental and physical realms. At its core, this connection illuminates how our thoughts, emotions, and beliefs influence our physical health and overall well-being.

Imagine this: Your breath is like a built-in stress relief button. In those frustrating traffic jams or stressful workdays, taking a few deep breaths can feel like hitting the reset button on your day. It's a simple practice that doesn't cost a thing, making it accessible to everyone.

Now, let's talk about physical activity. You don't need an expensive gym membership or fancy equipment. Picture yourself dancing to your favorite music in the comfort of your living room or enjoying a brisk walk-in a nearby park. These are not just affordable options; they are joyful ways to stay active and boost your mood.

Mindfulness can be as ordinary as doing your daily chores. Think about it - when your hands are busy washing dishes or folding laundry, you have an opportunity to practice mindfulness. It's about being fully present in the moment, finding beauty in simplicity, and easing stress without spending a dime.

Emotions play a vital role in our well-being. Remember the last time you had a hearty laugh with friends? That laughter not only lifted your spirits but also provided stress relief. On the flip side, bottling up negative emotions can lead to tension and discomfort. It's a reminder that our emotional well-being is as crucial as our physical health.

When it comes to resources, the internet is a treasure trove of free guidance. There are websites and YouTube channels offering guided meditations, workout routines, and emotional well-being exercises. It's like having a personal wellness coach at your fingertips, and it won't break the bank.

Creating a tranquil space for meditation or relaxation doesn't require expensive decor. A comfortable chair or cushion, soft lighting, and calming music (which can be found for free online) can suffice. It's about crafting an oasis of peace within your means.

Maintaining a balanced diet is a cornerstone of mind-body health. You don't have to empty your wallet at pricey health food stores. Consider buying in-season produce, cooking nutritious meals at home, and skipping those tempting, but unhealthy, processed snacks. Your budget and waistline will thank you.

Even in a bustling workplace, well-being is within reach. Short breaks for stress relief can be seamlessly integrated into your workday. Picture yourself discreetly stretching at your desk or taking a few moments for deep breathing. These tiny breaks are like mini vacations for your mind and body.

The mind-body connection's intricate facets invite us to explore its depths and harness its potential. By nurturing this connection through practices like breathwork, physical activity, and emotional well-being management, you empower yourself to unlock optimal health and well-being, all within your reach, regardless of your background or financial circumstances.

CHAPTER 24
The Science of Optimizing Nutrition

THE SCIENCE OF nutrition reveals the intricate interactions between food and our bodies, illuminating the path to optimal health and well-being. Food possesses the remarkable ability to serve as a form of medicine, nourishing our bodies and enhancing energy and focus. However, for many residing in urban areas, access to wholesome food options can be an ongoing challenge, hindering the pursuit of a nutritious diet.

A fundamental principle of leveraging food as medicine is to prioritize nutrient-dense, whole foods. These culinary treasures provide our bodies with vital vitamins, minerals, and antioxidants, essential for overall health and the prevention of chronic diseases.

Elevating the consumption of fruits and vegetables takes precedence, given their rich reserves of vitamins, minerals, and phytochemicals associated with reduced risks of chronic ailments such as heart disease, cancer, and diabetes. It's worth noting that the diversity of colors in your fruit and vegetable selection signifies a spectrum of nutrients. Dark leafy greens offer iron and calcium, while red and yellow produce abound in vitamin C and beta-carotene.

Simultaneously, prudent nutritional choices involve limiting the intake of processed foods, added sugars, and saturated fats. These dietary culprits, often brimming with empty calories and lacking essential nutrients, contribute to weight gain and chronic health conditions.

For those in colloquially termed "food deserts" their horizon is bleak. In these areas, fast food establishments and convenience stores (lacking produce or any real grocery department) typically reign supreme as primary food sources.

Addressing this challenge necessitates multifaceted solutions. Initiatives such as community gardens, farmers markets, and food co-ops can elevate access to fresh, locally sourced produce and other whole foods in inner city areas. Additionally, educational endeavors aimed at fostering nutritional awareness and guiding healthier food choices play a pivotal role. These efforts, encompassing cooking classes, nutrition education programs, and community outreach initiatives, empower individuals to make informed dietary decisions.

The science of nutrition examines the intricate interplay between food and our bodies, offering insights into the quest for optimal health and well-being. It sounds oversimplified, but truth is that by embracing nutrient-dense, whole foods while curbing the consumption of processed fare, added sugars, and saturated fats, we can harness the healing potential of food to nourish our bodies, amplify our energy levels, and sharpen our focus. However, for those grappling with limited access to healthy food options in urban environments, it is imperative that we continue to seek out and implement strategies aimed at enhancing accessibility and nutritional education.

Remember that your journey towards better health and well-being is a lifelong endeavor. Nourishing your body with the right foods isn't just a one-time effort; it's a path you walk every day.

Stay curious and open to new nutritional insights. Make informed choices about what you eat, read labels, and experiment with new recipes. Embrace the pleasures of mindful eating, savoring each bite, and paying attention to how different foods make you feel.

But also, be gentle with yourself. We all face challenges, whether it's navigating food deserts, handling dietary restrictions, or simply finding the time to prepare healthy meals. Remember that small, sustainable changes can lead to significant improvements in your health.

Most critically, never underestimate the power of community. Engage with others who share your nutritional goals, attend local farmers markets, and participate in nutrition education programs. Together, we can create a world where nutritious, whole foods are accessible to all, and where everyone has the knowledge and tools to nourish their bodies effectively.

The Future of Nutrition: Where Science Meets Possibility

Looking to the future, the field of nutrition is always evolving and good to keep an eye on. New discoveries emerge, and our understanding of the intricate relationship between food and our bodies deepens. Science offers exciting possibilities, from personalized nutrition plans based on genetics to innovative ways of addressing global nutritional challenges.

Stay informed about the latest developments in nutrition and remain adaptable in your approach to eating. As technology and research progress, we may uncover new ways to optimize our diets for health and longevity.

But amidst the advancements, remember that the core principles of nutrition remain unchanged. Whole, nutrient-dense foods will always be the foundation of a healthy diet. So, as you embrace the future of nutrition, keep your roots firmly planted in the wisdom of the past and the knowledge you've gained on this journey. With that, I wish you a future filled with vibrant health, energy, and a deep connection to the nourishing power of food. Your nutritional journey is a lifelong adventure, and I'm confident that you're well-equipped to embrace it with knowledge, passion, and purpose.

CHAPTER 25
The Science of Sleep

THE SCIENCE OF sleep is a captivating and ever-evolving field, shedding light on a profoundly intricate and intimate aspect of our lives. Throughout human history, sleep has been acknowledged as a cornerstone of well-being. In recent years, scientific revelations have deepened our understanding of its impact on cognition and physical health.

Central to comprehending sleep's significance is recognizing its role in memory consolidation. While we slumber, our brains diligently process and encode the day's events, cementing new knowledge for future use. This underscores the indispensability of a good night's sleep for learning and memory, and highlights the detrimental consequences of sleep deprivation on cognitive function.

But how can we enhance our sleep? Establishing a consistent sleep schedule proves to be one of the most effective strategies. Going to bed and waking up at roughly the same times each day helps regulate our internal body clocks, facilitating bedtime consistency. Additionally, nurturing a tranquil bedtime routine, which may involve reading or listening to soothing music, signals to the body that it's time to rest.

Crafting a comfortable sleep environment is equally pivotal. A dark, quiet, and pleasantly cool bedroom, furnished with a comfortable mattress and supportive pillows, sets the stage for restorative sleep. Additionally, avoiding stimulants like caffeine, nicotine, and alcohol before bedtime is essential, as they can disrupt the sleep cycle. Engaging in physical activity during the day can also improve sleep quality by reducing stress and anxiety.

Incorporating these crucial tips can further enhance your sleep quality:

1. **Sleep Hygiene Tips:** Practice sleep hygiene by keeping electronics out of the bedroom, avoiding heavy meals close to bedtime, and reducing caffeine intake during the day.

2. **Sleep Disorders:** Be aware of common sleep disorders like insomnia, sleep apnea, and restless leg syndrome, as understanding their signs and symptoms can help you identify potential issues.

3. **Technology and Sleep:** Recognize the impact of technology on sleep, particularly the importance of reducing screen time before bed due to the disruptive effects of blue light on melatonin production.

In my own sleep journey, I've experienced a direct correlation between the quality of my sleep and my daily performance. When I fall short on sleep, my day becomes foggy, and recalling information or performing at my peak becomes a challenge. However, on well-rested nights, I find a sense of clarity, enhanced well-being, and a feeling of being on top of the world. Sleep isn't just a routine for me, it's a vital component that exponentially improves my health.

While I haven't encountered significant sleep challenges, my passion for my work often tempts me to stay up late, reveling in the joys of my projects. Yet, I've come to realize the wisdom in Da Vinci's words, "A well-spent day brings happy sleep." It's a reminder to gracefully call it a night, knowing that a good night's sleep is an investment in the next day's success.

As I share these insights, I hope every reader will embrace the significance of sleep in their lives. Beyond the words on these pages, I encourage you to delve deeper, research, and explore additional ways to enhance your sleep quality. By doing so, you can unlock the potential for improved memory, heightened mental clarity, better health, and an overall elevated quality of life.

CHAPTER 26
Using Breathwork to Oxygenate the Body, Improve Lung Function, and Boost Energy

BREATHING IS AN essential bodily function often overlooked. Surveying the science of breathing, known as breathwork, reveals its profound impact on physical and mental well-being. Proper breathing techniques can oxygenate the body, enhance lung function, and boost energy levels. In this chapter, we explore the science of breathing and the advantages of breathwork, offering step-by-step guidance for five breath exercises.

The human body constantly craves oxygen for proper functioning. As we breathe, oxygen enters through the nose or mouth, travels to the lungs, and is distributed through the bloodstream. Sadly, many people have adopted unhealthy breathing habits, such as shallow chest breathing, leading to insufficient oxygen intake, and contributing to various health issues.

Breathwork is a technique that grants conscious control over our breath, amazingly benefiting your overall health and well-being. By mastering proper breathing, you can elevate oxygen levels in your body, enhance lung capacity, and boost vitality. Beyond the physical benefits, breathwork also serves as a powerful tool to alleviate stress, enhance sleep quality, and improve overall mental and physical wellness.

Breathing Exercises Promote Relaxation and Calmness

Through breathwork exploration, I uncovered a calmness within the chaos. Each technique offered rhythms of healing and tranquility within life's tumultuous-feeling labyrinth.

There are many breathwork exercises to explore and use as you need in various settings. In my experience, **Ujjayi Breathing**, with its soothing sound, mirrored my aspiration for peace amidst turmoil. Amid life's turbulence, the self-made white noise provided pockets of stillness.

Humming Bee Breath brought harmony between breath and tranquility. Amid life's turbulence, it granted profound moments of reprieve.

Relaxing Breath, like a bridge to stillness, flowed naturally within my hectic schedule. Inhales and exhales offered moments of respite amid the frenzy.

In the rhythm of my bustling life, I discovered that using the art of breathwork for healing and weaving solace into hectic moments is especially easy and effective.

Let's delve into five diverse breath exercises:

- **Diaphragmatic (Belly) Breathing:** Begin by comfortably sitting or lying down, placing one hand on your chest and the other on your stomach. Inhale slowly through your nose, allowing your abdomen to rise as your lungs fill with air. Exhale gradually through your mouth, feeling your stomach fall. Dedicate several minutes to this exercise, focusing on your diaphragmatic movement as you breathe.

- **Box Breathing:** Find a relaxed position and inhale through your nose for a count of four. Hold your breath for a count of four, then exhale through your mouth for another count of four. Once more, hold your breath for a count of four. Repeat this rhythmic pattern for several minutes to attain balance and relaxation.

- **Alternate Nostril Breathing:** Sit or lie down comfortably. You are going to use your right thumb to close your right nostril and your ring finger to close your left nostril. Begin by closing your left nostril and breathing through your right nostril, then close the right side with your thumb and exhale through the left side. Switch to the opposite side, inhaling through the left nostril, closing it, and exhaling through the right. Alternate between nostrils, practicing this technique for several minutes.

- **Lion's Breath:** Sit or lie down in a comfortable position, taking a deep breath in. Then, open your mouth wide, extend your tongue outward, and exhale with a prolonged "ha" sound, allowing any tension or stress to dissipate.

- **4-7-8 Breathing:** In any comfortable position, create a cadence of inhaling your breath for four counts, then hold for seven counts, and exhaling for eight counts. Allow your deliberate rhythm to build a sanctuary of poise.

By incorporating these breath exercises into your daily routine, you can harness the power of breathwork to enhance your well-being, manage stress, and cultivate a deeper connection between your body and mind. Remember that the simple act of conscious breathing can be a transformative force in your life, providing vitality and clarity while promoting overall health.

CHAPTER 27
The Healing Art of Hand Mudras

THE HEALING ART of hand mudras is an ancient practice that involves using specific finger positions to promote physical and mental well-being. Mudras are hand gestures or positions that are believed to stimulate different energy centers in the body, leading to a variety of health benefits. These finger positions can be used with a meditation or as a standalone practice. In this chapter, we will explore the science of hand mudras, their historical origins, and the profound benefits they offer. Additionally, I will provide step-by-step instructions for eight different hand mudra exercises to empower you on your journey to improved health and well-being.

The practice of hand mudras dates back thousands of years and is believed to have originated in India. Mudras are considered a powerful tool for harnessing the body's energies and facilitating a connection between the physical and spiritual realms. By practicing hand mudras, you can influence and balance the energy in your body, which is thought to contribute to improved physical and mental well-being.

Hand mudras offer a myriad of health benefits, addressing various aspects of your overall wellness. For instance, the Gyan mudra, where the tip of the index finger touches the thumb, is believed to enhance concentration and memory. The Prana mudra, connecting the tip of the little finger to the thumb, is thought to invigorate energy levels and bolster the immune system. Meanwhile, the Shuni mudra, where the tip of the middle finger meets the thumb, is associated with stress reduction and a sense of tranquility.

Let's delve into the transformative potential of hand mudras by exploring eight distinct mudra exercises, being careful to note the placement at the tip or base of the finger.

1. **Prana Mudra:** Boost your energy levels and fortify your immune system. Sit comfortably, rest your hands on your knees, and connect the tip of your little finger to your thumb. Concentrate on your breath while maintaining this mudra for several minutes.

2. **Shuni Mudra:** Cultivate calmness and alleviate stress. Sit in a comfortable position, hands resting on your knees, and touch the tip of your middle finger to your thumb. Let your breath guide you as you hold this mudra for several minutes.

3. **Apana Mudra:** Improve digestion and elimination. Sit comfortably, hands on your knees, and bring the tip of your ring finger to your thumb. Focus on your breath while maintaining this mudra for several minutes.

4. **Surya Mudra:** Enhance metabolism and vitality. Find a comfortable sitting position, rest your hands on your knees, and connect the tip of your ring finger to the base of your thumb. Concentrate on your breath while holding this mudra for several minutes.

5. **Varuna Mudra:** Promote hydration and skin health. Sit comfortably, hands resting on your knees, and touch the tip of your little finger to the base of your thumb. Allow your breath to guide you as you maintain this mudra for several minutes.

6. **Vayu Mudra:** Enhance respiratory function and alleviate joint pain. Sit comfortably, hands on your knees, and bring the tip of your index finger to the base of your thumb. Focus on your breath while holding this mudra for several minutes.

7. **Akash Mudra:** Improve communication and self-expression. Find a comfortable sitting position, rest your hands on your knees, and connect the tip of your thumb to the base of your little finger. Let your breath be your guide as you maintain this mudra for several minutes.

8. **Gyan Mudra:** Enhance concentration and memory by placing your index finger's tip on your thumb while keeping the other fingers extended. Breathe deeply and hold this position, focusing on your breath for several minutes.

The healing art of hand mudras offers a profound pathway to holistic well-being. These ancient practices, rooted in tradition and enriched with wisdom, can empower you to achieve physical and mental balance. Incorporating hand mudras into your daily routine can be an effective and transformative approach to enhancing your overall health and well-being. Explore these mudra exercises with an open heart and mind, and embark on a journey of self-discovery and healing.

CHAPTER 28
The Power of Eye Movement: Using Eye Exercises to Improve Vision and Reduce Tension

THE EYES, OFTEN referred to as the windows to the soul, are a vital organ of the body, serving as our primary means of perceiving the world. However, in our modern digital age, prolonged screen time and daily stressors can lead to eye strain and fatigue. Fortunately, eye exercises offer a practical and effective means to enhance vision, alleviate stress and tension, and maintain overall eye health.

Eye Palming Exercise

The palming exercise is a simple yet powerful technique to relax the eyes and relieve tension. Begin by finding a comfortable seated position and gently close your eyes. Cup your hands over your closed eyes, ensuring there's no pressure on the eyes themselves. The warmth from your hands will gradually relax the muscles surrounding your eyes. In this darkness, focus on your breath and let the soothing darkness envelop you. Practice this exercise for several minutes to rejuvenate your eyes.

Read more about palming in *Natural Vision Improvement* by Janet Goodrich.

Eye Rotation Exercise

The eye rotation exercise is designed to strengthen the eye muscles and enhance vision. While seated comfortably, close your eyes. Slowly, in a clockwise direction, rotate your eyes for several minutes. Then, switch to a counterclockwise rotation for the same duration. Repeat this exercise several times daily to promote eye muscle flexibility and vision improvement.

Read more about eye rotations in *The Bates Method for Better Eyesight Without Glasses* by William H. Bates, M.D..

Eye Focus Shift Exercise

The focus shift exercise aims to sharpen your ability to focus and concentrate. Sit comfortably and extend your arm, holding a pen or pencil at arm's length. Focus your gaze on the pen or pencil. Gradually bring it closer to your nose while maintaining your focus. As the object approaches your nose, swiftly shift your focus to the background. Repeat this exercise multiple times throughout the day to enhance your concentration skills.

Read more about focus shifting in *Improve Your Vision Without Glasses or Contact Lenses* by Steven M. Beresford.

Eye exercises are a valuable tool for preserving and improving eye health. Regular practice can help prevent eye strain, alleviate stress-related symptoms, and enhance visual acuity, allowing you to enjoy the world with clarity and comfort. By incorporating these exercises into your daily routine, you empower yourself to maintain optimal eye health and overall well-being.

CHAPTER 29
Mastering Body Poses for Posture Improvement and Pain Reduction

MAINTAINING GOOD POSTURE is crucial for overall health and well-being. Proper body positioning not only reduces pain but also boosts confidence. In this chapter, we will explore various body postures that can enhance your posture and overall physical and mental health.

The Benefits of Good Posture

Incorporating good posture into your daily life offers numerous physical and mental benefits. Enhanced circulation and reduced muscular stress occur when proper alignment allows muscles to work efficiently, reducing strain on joints and minimizing pain, especially in the back, neck, and shoulders. When our posture is strong, our lungs expand fully, enhancing lung function and increasing energy levels.

It is well known that good posture can enhance our appearance by making you appear taller, slimmer, and more confident. Overall improved mental well-being comes when an upright posture boosts self-confidence, reduces anxiety and depression, and improves focus and concentration.

Here are ten yogic practices that encourage improving our posture:

- **Wonder Woman Posture:** Imagine standing just like her—tall, with feet hip-width apart and hands resting confidently on your hips. Visualize a string from the top of your head gently pulling you upward. This posture exudes confidence and strength.

- **Superhero Posture:** Similar to the Wonder Woman stance, with a wide stance place one foot slightly ahead of the other. Imagine you're ready to take flight, radiating confidence and strength.

- **Mountain Pose:** Stand tall with feet hip-width apart, arms extended upward as if reaching for the stars. This posture improves balance and grounds you.

- **Downward Dog Pose:** Begin from a hands-and-knees position, then lift your hips upward, forming an inverted V-shape. This stretch benefits the entire body, particularly the spine and shoulders.

- **Cobra Pose:** Lie on your stomach with your hands beside your chest. Gradually raise your head, chest, and arms while keeping your elbows close to your body. This posture strengthens the back and shoulders.

- **Child's Pose:** Sit back on your heels, lean forward, and stretch your arms out in front of you. This relaxation posture helps release tension throughout your body.

- **Warrior Pose:** Stand tall with one foot ahead of the other and raise your arms above your head. This posture builds strength in the legs and arms.

- **Tree Pose:** Stand tall, placing one foot on the inside of the opposite thigh, pressing the sole into the thigh. This pose enhances balance and stability.

- **Seated Forward Bend:** Sit with legs straight, then slowly lean forward, reaching for your toes. This posture stretches the entire back of the body and eases back and shoulder tension.

- **Cat and Cow Stretch:** Start in a hands-and-knees

position. Inhale while arching your back like a cat and exhale while rounding your spine. This posture stretches the entire spine and eases back tension.

Remember that consistency is key when aiming for posture improvement. Everyone's body is unique, so be mindful of discomfort during these exercises, and consider consulting a yoga instructor if needed. Listen to your body, avoid pushing too hard, and focus on deep, slow breaths to maximize the benefits of these poses.

Consistently being mindful of your posture throughout the day and integrating these exercises into your routine can improve your overall health and well-being.

CHAPTER 30
The Healing Magic of Self-Massage: Reducing Stress, Tension, and Boosting Circulation

SELF-MASSAGE, AN AGE-OLD practice with roots in ancient civilizations such as China, Egypt, and Greece, is a recognized method for reducing stress, tension, and enhancing circulation within the body. While we may think of massage solely as a therapeutic resource that needs to be applied by another party, such as a family member or health professional, you will be amazed at the healing measures self-massage provides.

The Benefits of Self-Massage

- **Stress and Tension Reduction:** Self-massage triggers the release of endorphins, natural mood-enhancing and pain-relieving chemicals. It relaxes muscles and relieves tension, resulting in reduced pain and discomfort.
- **Improved Circulation:** Self-massage promotes better blood and oxygen flow to muscles, enhancing overall health. It also supports lymphatic circulation, vital for waste and toxin removal from the body.
- **Enhanced Skin Appearance:** Increased blood flow from self-massage can lead to improved skin tone and

reduced wrinkles and fine lines. It stimulates collagen production, vital for skin elasticity.

- **Increased Range of Motion and Flexibility:** Self-massage releases muscle tension and stiffness, enhancing mobility and flexibility, which can alleviate pain caused by tight muscles.

Self-Massage Exercises

As with other healing mindfulness practices, you can enjoy the convenience and benefit of these five self-massage exercises at any time throughout your day:

- **Hand and Finger Massage:** Gently massage each finger with your thumb, starting at the tip and moving towards the base to relieve hand and finger tension.
- **Foot Massage:** Use your hands to massage the soles of your feet, especially focusing on the heels and toes for complete foot relaxation.
- **Scalp Massage:** Employ your fingertips in circular motions to gently massage your scalp, relieving head and neck tension.
- **Abdominal Massage:** With clockwise motions, use your hands to massage your abdomen, promoting digestion and tension release.
- **Shoulder and Neck Massage:** Gently knead and massage your shoulders and neck to alleviate tension and stiffness.

Remember to apply moderate pressure and avoid painful or inflamed areas during self-massage.

Incorporating self-massage into your daily routine can significantly enhance your physical and mental well-being. By practicing these techniques regularly, you can promote relaxation and overall health, allowing you to fully enjoy the benefits of self-massage.

SECTION III
Reaching Higher States Through Advanced Practices

CHAPTER 31
Cultivating Inner Peace
in the Midst of Urban Chaos

MASTERING INNER PEACE is an ongoing journey that demands patience, practice, and a willingness to explore new paths to serenity. It transcends mere silence; it's a state of mind that can be nurtured amid the clamor of a city.

The Power of Mindfulness Meditation

One tried-and-true method for discovering inner peace amidst urban chaos is mindfulness meditations. This practice entails attentiveness to the present moment, embracing it without judgment. It can alleviate stress, anxiety, enhance concentration, and foster an enduring sense of inner peace. Scientific studies even demonstrate its potential to reshape the brain, boosting gray matter in areas linked to attention and self-regulation.

The Practice of Street Meditation

In some Asian cultures, individuals engage in "street meditation" or "urban mindfulness." This approach acknowledges that the mind can be trained to stay present, unfazed by external distractions. By immersing themselves in the sensory richness of bustling streets and markets, people can unearth inner peace and tranquility amidst the urban pandemonium. The simplest way to do this is to name each object that passes your vision without any judgment or additional information. For instance, as the traffic flows by, within your head you will note "truck," "car," "car," "motorcycle," and so on. Within a short time, you will feel an internal shift towards a more relaxed state.

Creating a Quiet Space Within

An alternative strategy for finding inner peace in a noisy city involves carving out a "quiet space" within yourself. By closing your eyes and centering your awareness on your breath, reciting a mantra, or spending a few moments visualizing a serene location, you can divert your attention from external chaos to the present moment. This shift can elevate feelings of inner peace and overall well-being.

The Role of Physical Exercise

Physical exercise, too, can be a gateway to inner peace. It effectively reduces stress, enhances well-being, and promotes relaxation. Engaging in regular exercise can create a solid foundation for inner peace amid the hustle and bustle. Occidental urban cultures often reflect their intense, revved-up lifestyles in the idealized forms of physical exercise they tout: high intensity training, cardio, and strength and weight training. While the body and mind undoubtedly need these forms of exercise, can you recall peaceful images of large groups of people and individuals in parks doing Asian exercises such as Qi Gong,

Tai Chi, or yoga? Healing movement also needs to be gentle and mindful. Try some gentler exercises to create a mind-body connection that encourages inner peace.

Wisdom Teachings for Inner Peace

In addition to the above strategies, there are ancient practices crossing cultures which we can call "wisdom teachings." These practices usually have a well-known maxim that sums up the concept. Wisdom teachings offer invaluable insights to find inner peace in the urban jungle.

- **The Art of Letting Go:** Release negative thoughts, emotions, and judgments to clear the mental clutter that obstructs inner peace.
- **Embracing Non-Attachment:** Avoid excessive fixation on specific outcomes, which can lead to frustration when plans go awry. Embrace the serenity of detachment.
- **The Power of Acceptance:** Accept life as it unfolds, relinquishing the constant urge to have control. Inner peace can thrive in the face of uncertainty.
- **Cultivate Gratitude:** Shift your focus to what you have rather than what you lack. Gratitude directs attention away from external turmoil toward the present moment.
- **The Compassion Connection:** Extend kindness and understanding to yourself and others. Practicing compassion nurtures the inner peace that you are resonating within and extending outward.

Cultivating inner peace is a journey marked by patience, practice, and a willingness to explore new realms of self-awareness. With dedication and persistent effort, inner peace can thrive in any environment, including the heart of a noisy city.

Inner peace isn't merely about seeking tranquility amidst

urban chaos; it's about nurturing a serene mind and heart. These wisdom teachings of "letting go," "non-attachment," "acceptance," "gratitude," and "compassion" serve as beacons guiding us towards inner peace, irrespective of external circumstances. Remember, the path to inner peace requires dedication, practice, and a continual willingness to explore new dimensions of being. With unwavering commitment, you will be pleasantly surprised that you can uncover inner peace and tranquility in any setting.

CHAPTER 32
Embracing Solitude: How to Harness the Healing Power of Alone Time

SOLITUDE, THE STATE of being alone, has a profound capacity to heal the body, mind, and spirit. In our fast-paced world, consumed by the demands of daily life, the importance of alone time often gets overshadowed. However, embracing solitude allows us to reconnect with ourselves, fostering a deeper sense of inner peace and well-being.

In the hustle and bustle of city life, finding moments of peace might seem like a rare gem. Sure, we have libraries, bookstores, saunas, and parks as little sanctuaries in our cities offering a temporary break. But let me tell you a secret. The real magic happens when you learn to create solitude within yourself, right in the midst of the chaos. It's not about escaping to some tranquil hideaway, it's about carrying a slice of quiet within your own being.

Imagine this, you're surrounded by honking horns, flashing lights, and the ever-present collective sounds of city noise, yet there you are, calm as a cucumber. This is no Jedi mind trick, it's the art of inner solitude. I promise that you can master this skill, no matter where you find yourself. So yes, embrace those short bursts of calm in the library or the park, but remember, the real zen sanctuary is right within you, waiting to be discovered in the midst of city chaos.

It's important to distinguish solitude from loneliness.

Loneliness stems from a lack of connection with others and is a negative emotion. In contrast, solitude is a positive state that can be experienced even in the presence of others. Intentional solitude is a time for reflection, introspection, and self-discovery, an opportunity to nurture our inner selves, tap into our intuition, and find answers within.

There are immense benefits to reveling in solitude, including:

- The Healing Power of Solitude

One of the most profound benefits of solitude is its ability to recharge our batteries. When we spend time alone, we disconnect from the distractions of daily life, allowing us to refuel physically and emotionally. This rejuvenation provides the energy and focus we need to navigate life's demands and heal from life's traumas.

- Reconnecting with the Self

Another remarkable aspect of solitude is its capacity to help us reconnect with our inner selves. By turning our attention inward during alone time, we can delve into our thoughts, feelings, and emotions. This process aids in self-understanding, personal growth, and informed decision-making.

- A Path to Self-Discovery

Solitude serves as a powerful tool for self-discovery. Time spent alone allows us to explore our inner selves, uncovering our strengths, weaknesses, values, and life's purpose.

Taking Inspiration from Famous Figures

Many people who are well-known for their wisdom and talent have attested to the transformative power of solitude. One such luminary is Maya Angelou, the celebrated author, poet, and civil rights activist. She often sought solitude to reflect and write, crediting it with helping her find her unique voice as a writer. "I write, for myself, for my own pleasure, for the pleasure of others, and I write to hear that voice, to transcribe it," Angelou once said.

The African American author and poet Langston Hughes also found solace in alone time, viewing it as essential for finding his voice as a writer. "I shall sit and work, work, work, until the voice of the inner self is heard," Hughes proclaimed.

Ralph Waldo Emerson, a philosopher and thinker, echoed their sentiments. Like Angelou and Hughes, Emerson valued solitude as a means of personal growth and self-discovery.

Solitude: A Personal Journey

I've discovered that this daily ritual, which may seem counterintuitive for an extrovert, plays a crucial role in my overall well-being. It allows me to escape from the constant influx of external stimuli, giving my mind the rest it deserves. In the solitude of my space, I find a respite from the images and information forced upon us by society.

As I sit in quiet contemplation, I've learned to listen to my inner voice, a voice that often gets drowned out in the noise of daily life. This connection with my inner self helps me understand my thoughts, feelings, and emotions better, paving the way for more informed decisions. One significant advantage of solitude is its positive impact on my stress levels. The break from the chaos of everyday life leads to a reduction in cortisol levels, the body's stress hormone. In contrast, it encourages the release of endorphins, the body's natural mood lifters. During these moments of solitude, I often find myself in a serene mental space, far from the stressors that can occupy my mind.

Moreover, this daily dose of solitude fuels my creativity. It's my canvas, my meditation cushion, and my stage for self-discovery. Here, I've had some of my most innovative ideas. It's where I curate art that I later showcase at venues or sell, crafting the kind of life I desire.

Incorporating Solitude into Daily Life

There are various ways to practice solitude. Allocate time each day, whether it's a few minutes or a few hours, for solitude. You can achieve this by taking a contemplative walk in nature, practicing meditation, or simply sitting in silence. Disconnecting from technology and social media also fosters mindfulness and self-connection.

My advice for anyone seeking to harness the healing power of solitude is to manage your time wisely. Carve out a pocket of your day to spend with yourself. Learn what makes you uniquely you. In this precious alone time, you can build yourself into an amazing version of yourself.

CHAPTER 33
Self-Love: Generating Love Within and Vibrating it Outward

Love is one of the most powerful emotions that we can experience as human beings. It can heal, transform, and uplift us, not only in our relationships with others but also in our relationship with ourself. In this chapter, we will explore the practice of generating love within ourselves and vibrating it out into the world. We will also examine the neuroscientific benefits of this practice, as well as the benefits of what we can manifest from it.

My Love-Fueled Journey

One of the first steps in generating love within us is to develop a deeper understanding of what love truly is. Love is not just a feeling or an emotion, but it is also a state of being. It is a vibration that we can cultivate within ourselves, and when we do, it can transform our entire being.

For me, all love begins with self-love. In my journey of generating more self-love, my process delves deep into my quest for understanding. I could not simply begin to love myself; I needed to unlearn what society told me about who I was. Amidst the barrage of messages from movies, music, and media, navigating the tensions between different ethnicities in America, especially as an African-American, became a journey of self-discovery.

I found myself standing at the crossroads of my culture, challenged to unravel the truths about my identity from a biological, mental, and physical standpoint. Learning not only about the positive history and contributions of African-Americans, but embracing the rich tapestry of all people was a pivotal turning point. Realizing that I am no less than anyone else fueled a tremendous increase in my ability to self-love.

It's essential to note that self-love was instilled in my upbringing; it was a cornerstone in my household. However, the continuous process of research, digging into my roots, and understanding the multifaceted aspects of my identity contribute to my daily growth of self-love. This journey isn't just about affirmations; it's about uncovering and embracing the profound layers of my identity with a love that expands every day.

Central to self-love is prioritizing self-care and being kind to myself. Without this foundation, how could I navigate the challenges of this world and thrive as I have for decades? To sustain this joyful journey, I've learned to care for myself physically, emotionally, and spiritually. It means treating myself with kindness and compassion and forgiving myself when mistakes happen. Letting go of past hurts has been liberating.

The Science of Love

The neuroscientific benefits of a self-love practice are numerous. When we practice self-love and generate love within ourselves, the brain releases oxytocin, also known as the "love hormone." Oxytocin is linked to feelings of trust, generosity, and compassion. It also plays a role in reducing stress and anxiety and promoting feelings of relaxation and well-being.

When I radiate love into the world, it's a reciprocal journey.

Happy people make others happy, and I've adopted this as my way of life. The law of good for good is my belief – I give so that I can receive. When I serve others, I treat them how I'd want to be served. This practice has helped me forge meaningful connections, meet and keep friends, and contribute to my community's well-being.

Daily Practices for Cultivating Love

To generate love within ourselves and share it with the world, daily practices are essential. Here are six steps to help you cultivate love within yourself and radiate it out into the world:

1. **Practice self-care:** Prioritize your physical, emotional, and spiritual well-being. Eat well, exercise, sleep enough, and indulge in relaxation to fuel your self-love.

2. **Journaling:** Reflect on your thoughts and feelings daily. Use journaling to understand yourself better, identify areas for self-love growth, and process emotions.

3. **Meditation:** Embrace meditation to calm your mind and nurture inner peace and love. Different forms, like mindfulness and loving-kindness meditations, can be powerful tools.

4. **Gratitude:** Daily gratitude practice shifts your focus from scarcity to abundance, fostering love and positivity.

5. **Acts of Kindness:** Small acts of kindness to others amplify self-love. Holding the door open, offering help, acknowledging others with a small or nod – these simple actions radiate love.

6. **Visualization:** Create a mental picture of the love and positivity you desire in your life. Imagine yourself surrounded by love, and it can manifest into reality.

Remember, the path to self-love is a journey, not a

destination. Be patient and kind to yourself; perfection is not the goal.

By incorporating these practices into your daily life, you can begin to generate love within yourself and radiate it out into the world. This can help to improve your relationships with others, as well as your overall sense of well-being and happiness. Love truly is one of the most powerful emotions that we can experience as human beings, so let's make it a daily practice to cultivate it within ourselves and share it with the world.

CHAPTER 34
Cultivating Gratitude, Even in Tough Times

WE TALKED ABOUT gratitude earlier in Section I, however, I want to bring it back here and dive in a bit deeper. Gratitude, the practice of being thankful for the blessings in our lives, is a powerful tool that can help us navigate even the toughest of times. When life seems to be falling apart, finding reasons to be grateful can be challenging, yet it's during these moments that gratitude becomes essential for our well-being and growth.

Shifting Our Perspective Through Gratitude

Practicing gratitude offers us a profound shift in perspective. It's all too easy to get caught up in a negative spiral of thoughts and emotions, especially when facing adversity. However, by actively seeking out things to be thankful for, we can break that cycle and gain a more positive outlook on life.

But what about the difficult moments, the times when it feels like nothing is going our way? Why should we be grateful for the bad things that happen? It might seem counterintuitive, but these challenging experiences can be some of the most valuable and transformative lessons in our lives. They have the power to foster growth and teach us important life lessons. They can also help us appreciate the good things in our lives even more.

The Physical and Mental Benefits of Gratitude

Beyond its impact on our perspective, practicing gratitude has been scientifically proven to have significant effects on our physical and mental health. Studies have shown that individuals who regularly practice gratitude experience lower levels of stress, anxiety, and depression. Additionally, they tend to have better overall physical health. This is because gratitude activates positive emotions in the brain, leading to a profound improvement in our overall well-being.

Cultivating Gratitude Daily

Cultivating gratitude requires consistent effort, especially during challenging times. One powerful way to do this is by keeping a gratitude journal. Each day, take a moment to reflect on the things you're grateful for, no matter how small they may seem. It could be as simple as having a roof over your head or having a friend to talk to. By consciously focusing on these aspects of our lives, we can begin to see the world in a different light, even when it appears bleak.

My Personal Gratitude Practice

I can personally attest to the transformative power of gratitude. Each morning, I make it a point to wake up and intentionally feel gratitude and appreciation for everything I can think of, even the things we often take for granted. For instance, I reflect on things like having roads to travel, a comfortable bed, a warm bath, health, and even the ability to think critically. I reflect on how many people around the world don't have the basic comforts. I ponder the knowledge and practices I've been blessed with. I find a quiet moment to sit in an upright meditation position and spend at least ten minutes focusing on gratitude before I start my day. This practice has made a tremendous positive difference in my thinking and my life.

Finding Hidden Opportunities in Challenges

Another approach is to seek hidden opportunities within difficult situations. For example, when faced with job loss, it can be an opportunity to explore new career paths or concentrate on personal growth. By seeking the positive aspects in challenging situations, we can shift our mindset and develop a genuine sense of gratitude.

Mindfulness and Gratitude

Mindfulness, the practice of being fully present in the moment without judgment, is another powerful way to cultivate gratitude, especially during tough times. It enables us to observe our thoughts and emotions without becoming entangled in them, offering a sense of clarity and perspective.

My Acts of Kindness and Gratitude

Acts of kindness play a significant role in my gratitude practice. I believe that by performing acts of kindness, we shift our focus from our own problems and concerns to the needs of others. This can be incredibly powerful in helping us see the world in a different light and find reasons to be grateful even when things are tough.

For me, one of the most fulfilling acts of kindness is teaching trades to young men in the inner city, helping them learn how to provide a quality life for themselves. I appreciate this opportunity more than almost anything. It's a blessing to me to be selfless and think about the welfare of our youth and others in need by employing them, not just for personal gain. Even during times that we didn't make significant profits, I am driven to create jobs. If it means having them work on my properties or taking on small client jobs that they could handle themselves, allowing them to keep the profit—these acts of kindness are deeply rewarding, and fill me with a profound sense of appreciation.

The Journey of Cultivating Gratitude

It's essential to remember that cultivating gratitude is a journey, not a destination. There may be days when it feels impossible to find anything to be grateful for, especially in the midst of adversity. During these moments, it's crucial to be kind to yourself and acknowledge that it's okay to struggle. Developing a consistent practice of gratitude takes time and patience.

Incorporating acts of kindness and mindfulness into your daily routine can be effective ways to cultivate gratitude, even during difficult times. Remember that gratitude's power lies in its ability to transform our perspective, improve our physical and mental health, and facilitate valuable insight and growth. It's a practice worth nurturing, for even in the darkest hours, gratitude can illuminate our path forward.

CHAPTER 35
The Art of No: How to Set Healthy Boundaries with Toxic People

AS WE DELVE into the art of setting healthy boundaries, let's take a moment to reflect on the importance of this practice. Boundaries are not merely lines drawn in the sand; they are vital shields that protect our well-being and sanity. We often learn this the hard way, as I did when I embraced my Islamic faith in the early '90s.

Back then, I was overjoyed to be among fellow believers, believing that our shared faith would guarantee harmonious relationships. However, reality soon taught me a different lesson. While the majority of my fellow believers were kind-hearted and genuine, a tiny few exhibited toxic behavior. This small minority clouded my early experiences and led me to believe that faith alone couldn't ensure healthy connections. It was a tough realization, but it was also an enlightening one. I came to understand that genuine companionship transcends titles of faith. It's about surrounding oneself with individuals who live by the principles of goodness and righteousness, individuals who strive to embody the essence of their beliefs.

These insights shaped my journey as I continued to explore the art of boundaries. The struggles and lessons I encountered felt like stepping into a vivid museum of life experiences. It was as if I had been walking through these exhibits, absorbing the stories and art around me. The pain in their eyes, the hurt on their faces—it all mirrored my own battles. I had allowed toxic people to control my life, and I was paying the price.

But amidst these challenges, I found hope. I wasn't alone in my struggles. The power of boundaries became evident, a force to protect me from the toxicity that had once engulfed me. Spending hours reflecting on these lessons, I absorbed insights into different boundary types and how to set them effectively. I discovered the importance of self-care and the empowerment of using my own voice to assert myself.

As I left this metaphorical museum of life experiences, I carried with me a newfound sense of empowerment. I had the tools to set healthy boundaries with the toxic people in my life. I could take control and protect myself from harm. Hope filled my heart, knowing that I could make the necessary changes.

Walking into the sunshine, I felt the weight lifting from my shoulders. A challenging road lay ahead, but I was prepared for the journey. I was ready to set healthy boundaries and take control of my life.

I knew I would carry these personal lessons with me, guiding me through the challenges that lay ahead:

Eight Lessons That Changed My Life

1. **Identify the Toxic Behavior:** Before setting boundaries, it's crucial to identify the specific toxic behaviors. This clarity helps in setting clear and specific boundaries.
2. **Communicate Clearly:** When setting boundaries, use "I" statements like "I need" or "I want" to communicate clearly, rather than "you should" or "you need to."
3. **Be Consistent:** After setting a boundary, consistently enforce it. Stand firm and don't allow toxic individuals to cross that boundary again.
4. **Be Prepared for Pushback:** Setting boundaries with

toxic people can be met with resistance and manipulation. Be prepared and have a plan to address it.

5. **Seek Support:** Setting boundaries with toxic individuals can be emotionally taxing. Build a support system, whether it's friends, family, or a therapist.

6. **Take Care of Yourself:** Remember that self-care is crucial. Make time for activities like exercise, hobbies, and spending time with loved ones.

7. **Be Realistic:** Understand that toxic people may not change, and you may need to limit or end the relationship entirely.

8. **Don't Blame Yourself:** Toxic people are responsible for their behavior; it's not your fault if they act harmfully.

Remember, setting healthy boundaries with toxic people is an ongoing process, requiring patience and persistence. Be kind to yourself and seek help if needed. With the right approach and support, you can take control of your life and create a safer, healthier environment. This experience is not unique to any particular faith; people from various backgrounds can relate to it, whether you are a Christian, Muslim, or follow any other religion.

SECTION IV
Appendix

Grab and Sit Meditation Exercises for Busy Lifestyles

Mindfulness Meditation Practices

WITHIN THE PAGES of this book, you have discovered a rich tapestry of meditation practices, each offering unique benefits for the mind, body, and spirit. I have cultivated these practices over years of study and travel, and they offer you a diverse range of tools to explore. Whether you seek enhanced focus, emotional healing, or a deeper connection with your inner self, these practices are here to support your journey.

The following are just a glimpse of the many meditation techniques that I have encountered and there are still more for all of us to learn. While exploring this curation of exercises, remember that meditation is a personal journey; you may find that one practice resonates with you more than others, while some just don't stick. That's perfectly normal and part of the beauty of the diversity of meditation. Enjoy your journey through the world of meditation and mindfulness. May it bring you peace and understanding on your path.

EXERCISE 1
Mindful Focus Meditation

These Mindful Focus Exercises are designed to help you cultivate mindfulness, improve your focus, and deepen your connection with the present moment. Practice them regularly, and you'll discover their transformative power in your daily life.

- -

Instructions:

1. Find a quiet and comfortable place to sit.
2. Close your eyes gently.
3. Take a deep breath in through your nose, and slowly exhale through your mouth.
4. Direct your attention to your breath, focusing on the sensation of the air entering and leaving your nostrils.
5. If your mind begins to wander, that's okay. When you notice it drifting, simply guide your focus back to your breath.
6. Continue this practice for 5-10 minutes every day.

Reflections:

1. What did you observe during this exercise?

   ____

   ____

2. How did your mind feel before and after the exercise?

   ____

   ____

3. How can you incorporate this practice into your daily life for improved focus and mindfulness?

   ____

   ____

- -

EXERCISE 2
Mindful Attention Worksheet

Instructions:

1. Take a moment to read each statement below.
2. Pause and reflect on each statement.
3. Jot down any thoughts, insights, or feelings that arise in the provided spaces.
4. Dedicate at least 15 minutes daily to complete this exercise.

Statements:

1. "My thoughts are like clouds in the sky, they come and go, but I am the sky."
2. "I am in control of my attention and can choose where to direct it."
3. "I can observe my thoughts without becoming attached to them."

Exercises for Cultivating Focus

As we are collectively losing our ability to focus in these technology-driven times, these exercises to cultivate your ability to focus are critical to incorporate into your healing journey. It's important to remember that building focus takes time and practice. When I was in meditation classes, many of my fellow students, including myself, faced challenges with our minds wandering away from the exercises at hand. This is entirely normal, and it's part of the learning process. Over time, with consistent practice, you'll find that your ability to focus will improve. Be patient with yourself and remember that progress is made one breath at a time.

These practices are just a starting point and can be modified to suit your individual needs and preferences. Feel free to explore other meditation techniques, such as mantra meditation or loving-kindness meditation, to find what resonates best with you on your journey of self-discovery.

EXERCISE 3
Focus with Time Limits

---

1. Select a task or activity that you will focus on for a set amount of time (e.g., reading a book, solving a math problem, drawing a picture).
2. Set a timer for 10 minutes.
3. Begin the task and focus your attention solely on that task for the entire 10 minutes.
4. Then take note of any distractions that arise and make a conscious effort to let them pass without acting on them.
5. Repeat the exercise, gradually increasing the time limit by 5 minutes each day.

10 Minute Fun Focus Game

An important skill to have in life, focus can be improved through some fun practices. The following game is designed to help you strengthen your focus and improve your ability to concentrate and stay on task for longer periods of time.

---

10 Minute Fun Focus Game

An important skill to have in life, focus can be improved through some fun practices. The following game is designed to help you strengthen your focus and improve your ability to concentrate and stay on task for longer periods of time.

Objective: The objective of this game is to practice focusing on a single task for a designated period of time.

- -

Instructions:

Choose a task or activity to focus on, such as reading a book, or working on a project. Set a timer for 10 minutes and focus on the task for that entire time. Once the timer goes off, take a break, and move onto the next activity.

Suggested Activities:

1. Read a book for 10 minutes.
2. Memorize a poem for 10 minutes.
3. Write a story for 10 minutes.
4. Solve a complex math problem for 10 minutes.
5. Draw a picture for 10 minutes.
6. Play a solo game for 10 minutes.
7. Practice a musical instrument for 10 minutes.
8. Practice a solo sport for 10 minutes.
9. Work on a project for 10 minutes.
10. Meditate for 10 minutes.

- -

By regularly playing this game of staying focused on a single task for a designated period, you will strengthen your focus and improve your ability to concentrate on tasks for longer periods of time.

15 Minutes of Fun Focus Game

When 10 minutes of focus games have become easier for you, it's time to work your brain muscles harder with these intermediate focus games.

Objective: The objective of the game remains to practice focusing on a single task for a designated period.

- -

Instructions:

Choose a task or activity below to focus on, this time set your timer for 15 minutes and then focus on the task for that entire time. Once the timer goes off, take a break, and move onto the next activity for as long as you can.

Activities:

1. Complete any project for 15 minutes.
2. Research a topic for 15 minutes.
3. Write a report or analysis of a current problem you are facing for 15 minutes.
4. Practice typing for 15 minutes.
5. Begin a project plan for 15 minutes.
6. Study for a test for 15 minutes.

- -

20 Minute Fun Focus Game

Here are some more suggestions to continue improving your focus through games.

Objective: The game's objective remains the same—to practice focusing on a single task for a designated period, but note that the time periods are increased.

- -

Instructions:

1. Choose a task or activity to focus on, especially one you have been avoiding, such as researching a topic or completing a project.
2. Set a timer for 20 minutes and concentrate on the task for the entire duration.
3. Once the timer goes off, take a break, and then proceed to the next activity.

Suggested Activities:

1. Complete a project for 20 minutes.
2. Practice a mindfulness meditation for 20 minutes.
3. Research a topic for 20 minutes.
4. Write a report, proposal, or summary for 20 minutes.
5. Practice typing for 20 minutes.
6. Plan a new project for 20 minutes.
7. Without doing anything else, listen to relaxing music for 20 minutes.
8. Practice a progressive muscle relaxation exercise for 20 minutes.
9. Read a difficult book for 20 minutes.
10. Work on a computer program for 20 minutes.

- -

EXERCISE 4
Immersive Focus Activities

By engaging in immersive activities, we can apply scientifically proven techniques to sustain our attention on a single task for a set time.

- -

Focus Through Movement

1. Choose a simple movement or exercise (e.g., stretching, a yoga pose, or a tai chi movement).
2. Focus on the movement, the sensation of your body, and your breath as you perform the movement.
3. Try to clear your mind of any other thoughts and focus only on the movement.
4. Repeat for 5-10 minutes each day, building up your practice to longer periods of time.

Focus Through Music

1. Choose a piece of music that you find calming and focus-inducing.
2. Listen to the music with headphones and close your eyes.
3. Try to clear your mind of any other thoughts and focus only on the intricacies of the music.
4. Repeat for 5-10 minutes each day, building up your practice to longer periods of time.

- -

Focus Through Nature

1. Find a quiet and peaceful spot in nature (e.g., a park, beach, or forest).
2. Sit or stand comfortably and focus on your surroundings.
3. Try to clear your mind of any other thoughts and focus only on the details of the nature around you.
4. Repeat for 5-10 minutes each day, building up your practice to longer periods of time.

Three Fundamental Meditation Practices

THE FOLLOWING SIMPLE, yet powerful meditation practices are like mini vacations for your mind. These exercises each offer a break from the daily hustle and a chance to connect with your inner calm. Whether you are new to meditation or a seasoned practitioner, these exercises are crafted to guide you on a path to serenity. As with all the exercises in this book, you may find some here that you prefer more than others. That's fine, just keep practicing.

Find a comfy spot, take a deep breath, and let's embark on a journey to harness the healing power of meditation together. Your mind and soul will appreciate this deep nourishment.

EXERCISE 5
Breathing Meditation

Instructions:

1. Find a quiet and comfortable place to sit. Close your eyes and take a deep breath in through your nose, filling your lungs with air.

2. Exhale slowly through your mouth, letting go of any tension or stress in your body.

3. Bring your attention to your breath and focus on the sensation of the breath entering and leaving your body. Notice the rise and fall of your chest and the sensation of the air passing through your nose or mouth.

4. As you breathe, count each inhale and exhale. For example, *inhale 1, exhale 1, inhale 2, exhale 2*, and so on. Continue counting to 10 and then start again from 1.

5. If your mind wanders, gently bring your attention back to your breath and your counting.

6. Continue this practice for 5-10 minutes. When you are finished, take a moment to notice any changes in your body and mind before opening your eyes.

EXERCISE 6
Body Scan Meditation

Instructions:

1. Find a quiet and comfortable place to sit. Close your eyes and take a deep breath in through your nose, filling your lungs with air.

2. Exhale slowly through your mouth, letting go of any tension or stress in your body.

3. Begin by focusing on the sensation of your feet. Notice any areas of tension or discomfort. As you inhale, imagine sending a wave of relaxation to your feet. As you exhale, imagine any tension or discomfort flowing out of your feet.

4. Slowly move your attention up your body, focusing on each area for a few breaths. Progress your focus upwards via your ankles, calves, knees, thighs, hips, stomach, chest, shoulders, arms, hands, neck, and head.

5. If your mind wanders, gently bring your attention back to the body part you were focusing on and continue to send relaxation to that area.

6. Continue this practice for 5-10 minutes. When you are finished, take a moment to notice any changes in your body and mind before opening your eyes.

EXERCISE 7
Visualization Meditation

- -

Instructions:

1. Find a quiet and comfortable place to sit. Close your eyes and take a deep breath in through your nose, filling your lungs with air.

2. Exhale slowly through your mouth, letting go of any tension or stress in your body.

3. Imagine yourself in a peaceful and relaxing place. This can be a real or imagined place. It could be a beach, a forest, a garden, or any other place that brings you peace and calm.

4. Take a moment to notice all the details of the place. Notice the colors, sounds, smells, and sensations. Imagine yourself walking around the place and taking it all in.

5. If your mind wanders, gently bring your attention back to the visualization and continue to take in the details of the place.

6. Continue this practice for 5-10 minutes. When you are finished, take a moment to notice any changes in your body and mind before opening your eyes.

- -

Six Steps to Heal Your Anxiety

ANAGING ANXIETY PRESENTS challenges, yet it doesn't have to remain insurmountable. Embracing these six steps empowers you to conquer anxiety and embrace a more contented, enriched existence.

1. **Identify Your Anxiety Triggers:** The first step to finding control over your anxiety is to identify the triggers that cause it. This can be anything from certain situations, people, or even certain emotions. Once you know what triggers your anxiety, it will be easier to find ways to manage it.

2. **Challenge Your Negative Thoughts:** Anxiety often comes from negative thoughts or beliefs. Taking time to challenge those thoughts can help you gain control of your anxiety. Ask yourself questions such as, "Is this thought really true?" or "What evidence do I have to support this thought?" This will help you to separate the truth from the lies and help you to gain control over your anxiety.

3. **Practice Self-Care:** Self-care is an essential part of building self-confidence and dealing with anxiety. Taking time to do things that make you feel relaxed and happy, like reading, going for a walk, or listening to music, can help to reduce your anxiety.

4. **Learn Relaxation Techniques:** Learning relaxation techniques such as deep breathing and progressive muscle relaxation can help to reduce the physical symptoms of anxiety. Taking time to practice these techniques can help you gain control over your anxiety.

5. **Seek Social Support:** Anxiety can make it difficult to connect with others, but having strong social support can help you manage your anxiety. Reach out to family and friends and let them know how you are feeling.

6. **Take Care of Your Body:** It is important to take care of your physical health when dealing with anxiety. Eating a balanced diet, getting regular exercise, and getting enough sleep can all help to reduce your anxiety.

Eight Hand Mudra Positions

H AND MUDRAS ARE hand gestures or positions that are believed to stimulate different energy centers in the body, leading to a variety of health benefits.

Here are eight hand mudras to include in your meditations or to use as a standalone practice:

1. **Prana Mudra:** Boost your energy levels and fortify your immune system. Sit comfortably, rest your hands on your knees, and connect the tip of your little finger to your thumb. Concentrate on your breath while maintaining this mudra for several minutes.

2. **Shuni Mudra:** Cultivate calmness and alleviate stress. Sit in a comfortable position, hands resting on your knees, and touch the tip of your middle finger to your thumb. Let your breath guide you as you hold this mudra for several minutes.

3. **Apana Mudra:** Improve digestion and elimination. Sit comfortably, hands on your knees, and bring the tip of your ring finger to your thumb. Focus on your breath while maintaining this mudra for several minutes.

4. **Surya Mudra:** Enhance metabolism and vitality. Find a comfortable sitting position, rest your hands on your knees, and connect the tip of your ring finger to the base of your thumb. Concentrate on your breath while holding this mudra for several minutes.

5. **Varuna Mudra:** Promote hydration and skin health. Sit comfortably, hands resting on your knees, and touch the tip of your little finger to the base of your thumb. Allow your breath to guide you as you maintain this mudra for several minutes.

6. **Vayu Mudra:** Enhance respiratory function and alleviate joint pain. Sit comfortably, hands on your knees, and bring the tip of your index finger to the base of your

thumb. Focus on your breath while holding this mudra for several minutes.

7. **Akash Mudra:** Improve communication and self-expression. Find a comfortable sitting position, rest your hands on your knees, and connect the tip of your thumb to the base of your little finger. Let your breath be your guide as you maintain this mudra for several minutes.

8. **Gyan Mudra:** Enhance concentration and memory by placing your index finger's tip on your thumb while keeping the other fingers extended. Breathe deeply and hold this position, focusing on your breath for several minutes.

Ten Posture Exercises
to Boost Confidence and Well-being

GOOD POSTURE ENHANCES our appearance by making you appear taller, slimmer and more confident. Overall improved mental well-being comes when an upright posture boosts self-confidence, reduces anxiety and depression, and improves focus and concentration.

Here are ten yogic practices that help improve posture:

1. **Wonder Woman Posture:** Imagine standing tall just like her, with feet hip-width apart and hands resting confidently on your hips. Visualize a string from the top of your head gently pulling you upward. This posture exudes confidence and strength.

2. **Superhero Posture:** Similar to the Wonder Woman stance, place one foot slightly ahead of the other. Imagine you're ready to take flight, radiating confidence and strength.

3. **Mountain Pose:** Stand tall with feet hip-width apart, arms extended upward as if reaching for the stars. This posture improves balance and grounds you.

4. **Downward Dog Pose:** Begin from a hands-and-knees position, then lift your hips upward, forming an inverted V-shape. This stretch benefits the entire body, particularly the spine and shoulders.

5. **Cobra Pose:** Lie on your stomach with your hands beside your chest. Gradually raise your head, chest, and arms while keeping your elbows close to your body. This posture strengthens the back and shoulders.

6. **Child's Pose:** Sit back on your heels, lean forward, and stretch your arms out in front of you. This relaxation posture helps release tension throughout your body.

7. **Warrior Pose:** Stand tall with one foot ahead of the

other and raise your arms above your head. This posture builds strength in the legs and arms.

8. **Tree Pose:** Stand tall, placing one foot on the inside of the opposite thigh, pressing the sole into the thigh. This pose enhances balance and stability.

9. **Seated Forward Bend:** Sit with legs straight, then slowly lean forward, reaching for your toes. This posture stretches the entire back of the body and eases back and shoulder tension.

10. **Cat and Cow Stretch:** Start in a hands-and-knees position. Inhale while arching your back like a cat and exhale while rounding your spine. This posture stretches the entire spine and eases back tension.

Unleash Your Mind's Potential

Let's do it together.

THE JOURNEY TOWARDS empowerment starts here, at The Motivational Museum. It's time to unleash your full potential, heal from within, and create the life you've always envisioned.

Join us in this transformative adventure — book a session, invite us to your space, and let's embark on this journey together.

Visit our website, motivationalmuseum.com, to discover our coaching services.

We're here to assist you in any way we can, offering one-on-one coaching to support your growth and well-being. Remember, you don't have to navigate this path alone. Together, we can explore the boundless possibilities of your inner world.

About the Author

KHALIL MUHAMMAD, A Detroit-based activist for over 15 years, pioneers events that challenge societal norms, fostering self-discovery and personal growth. As a multifaceted entrepreneur, art collector & curator, mindset mentor, and meditation instructor, Khalil works with individuals from all walks of life to improve their lives and empower themselves. His dedication to mental liberation shines through his comprehensive guide, *Meditate to Elevate: Harnessing Your Superpowers in a World of Chaos,* offering transformative meditation techniques, historical insights, holistic wellness practices, and healing exercises.

Email: themotivationalmuseum@gmail.com
Tik Tok: @Khalilheals
Website: www.MotivationalMuseum.com
YouTube: The Motivational Museum
IG: @colossal_poetry_lounge

At the heart of The Motivational Museum, an endeavor led by the visionary Khalil Muhammad, lies a unique fusion of inspiration and artistry. Beyond the realm of words, the museum brings a visual tapestry that speaks to the soul.

Khalil's curated collection of artworks isn't just a feast for the eyes; it's an invitation to explore the depths of creativity and introspection. With each stroke of color and every intricately woven narrative, the artworks tell stories of resilience, dreams, and transformation.

What's more, these pieces aren't confined to the museum's walls alone – they're available for rent, allowing individuals and event organizers to infuse spaces with a touch of motivational magic. Imagine hosting an event enveloped in the vibrant energy of these artworks, coupled with Khalil's powerful talks on healing, manifestation, and mindfulness.

The art becomes a visual companion to the words, enhancing the impact and fostering an environment of growth and inspiration. The Motivational Museum isn't just a place; it's a multisensory experience where art and motivation coalesce, sparking a symphony of empowerment and creativity.

Acknowledgements

I extend my heartfelt gratitude to the following individuals who have played a significant role in shaping my journey:

To all my teachers, from my earliest years through to the present day, who have imparted wisdom and knowledge that has guided me along this path. Your dedication to education and commitment to nurturing young minds have left an indelible mark on my life.

I am deeply grateful to my spiritual teachers, Imam Luqman Abdullah, Imam Siraj Wahhaj, Shaykh Abdur Rashied, Imam Mubarak Al Mubarak Hassan, and Imam Abdoulaye Ndaw, for their guidance, wisdom, and spiritual insights that have enriched my understanding and deepened my connection to faith.

To my favorite inspirational speakers, including Jim Rohn, Dr. Wayne Dyer, Rev Ike, Joseph Murphy, Neville Goddard, Dr. Joe Dispenza, Bob Proctor, Bruce Lipton, Tony Robbins, and countless others, thank you for sharing your wisdom, insights, and transformative teachings. Your words have inspired me, challenged me, and encouraged me to strive for greater heights.

I'm also forever grateful to one of my first life coaches who taught me so much, Yasmine Yasmine.

A special thank you to the countless editors who have worked on my writings over the past eight years, including my most recent ones at Book P ower Publishing, Zarinah El-Amin, and Brooke Benoit. Your expertise, guidance, and dedication to improving the quality of this work are deeply appreciated.

And to all my employees at KSCC Hardwood Floors who

have done excellent work, enabling me to free myself and focus on producing my writings, thank you tremendously.

I am profoundly thankful for all the good that I have learned from each of you. Your knowledge lives on through me, shaping my thoughts, actions, and contributions to the world.

Made in the USA
Columbia, SC
28 April 2024